MANAGEMENT AND DEVELOPMENT

A Psychological Approach

MANAGEMENT AND DEVELOPMENT

A PSYCHOLOGICAL APPROACH

SALIL KUMAR

GYAN
GYAN PUBLISHING HOUSE
NEW DELHI-110 002

ISBN 81-212-0444-5
Library of Congress Card No. 93-900309

Published in 1993 by
Gyan Publishing House
5 Ansari Road
New Delhi - 110 002

Composed by Refill Master, Paschim Vihar and
Printed at Goyal Offset Works, Delhi.

CONTENTS

Preface vii

SECTION I

1. Introduction 3
2. Management Development Training Approaches 8
3. Earlier Studies in Training and Management Development 28

SECTION II

4. Development of Hypothesis 81
5. Methodology 87
6. Development of Scale 99

SECTION III

7. Results and Discussion 119
8. Conclusions and Recommendations 160
9. Limitations of the Study and Suggestions for Future Research 164

Bibliography 166

Index 190

PREFACE

The concept of Human Resources Development has emerged as a new field in the last decade and has gained greater concern. The Human Resource Development (HRD) aims at developing a variety of competencies and developing a culture in the organisation to utilize these competencies and contribute to organizational growth. It is important to view HRD as a continuous process. One of the most important means to bring about Organizational Development (OD) and in the broader context HRD is training and especially training for Management Development (MD). It is therefore relevant to develop managers through training who are the individual differences also play an important role. MD training and research has not been viewed to have impact of psychological factors and individual differences among managers, more so in the Government sector organizations. The corporate organisations were thought to strengthen the backbone of Indian economy through industrialization in order to support and provide necessary competition to the private sector for industrial growth and development after Independence. Unfortunately, the public sector organization have not displayed the desired level of results and many of such organizations fall into the category of heavy-loss incurring sick organizations / units imposing tough situations and serious problems for the Government. Training for MD and, in turn, optimizing HRD in the public sector organizations has not been considered important whereas, in fact, MD through training is crucially important to tackle such problems as are posed by the public sector enterprises.

It is in this context that it was planned to study some psychological correlates of management development especially in the training process. Evidences are that there is a definite impact of psychological factors, personality make up and individual differences of managers on their training experience. The investigation had been designed to study the impact of Occupational Aspiration, Job Involvement, Quality of Work Life, Job Satisfaction, Motivating Potential and Achievement Value on perception of training experiences of managers who received training in two different training organizations. The managers worked in two Government sector organizations although their nature of work differed, their basic function was to manage.

The result established that there was definitely an impact of psychological variables on the training experience of managers. It was also established that training experience could be predicted by the psychological correlates. The implication of this investigation directly suggest need for design of training modules for M.D. in more meaningful and enriching experiences to facilitate personal growth and development of managers. The results highlighted that to a great deal the training modules will be determined on the type of trainees. The model proposed in the study gets support by the results and the study has explained the Humanistic-Organismic perspective for designing future training programmes and MD/HRD strategies in organizations. The current thrust of the Humanistic-Organismic perspective gives rise to the concept of wholesome development of managers as individuals first, to become effective managers and change agents for HRD. The perception, attitude, motivation and personal growth and development are some important processes which require adequate consideration. These psychological processes and the psychological variables considered under the study are relevant to design of training for MD giving due regard to individual differences and personality characteristics of the managers. The views expressed in this book by the author are exclusively his own and not of the institute to which be belongs.

This work has been divided into three sections to manage the theoretical orientations and huge volume of research being condensed to provide the readers a composite picture of what has been the solution to various problems experienced and attempt made to find out possible solutions in India and abroad in Management Development.

I am highly indebted to Dr. Anuradha Sharma, Assistant Professor, Department of Humanities and Social Sciences, I.I.T., New Delhi and deeply grateful to Professor Kuldip Kumar, head Department of Field Units, NCERT, New Delhi for their able guidance, affectionate encouragement and critical suggestions which went a long way in providing the necessary insight into the problem and directed the course of study. I wish to thank Dr. Avnish Singh, then Research Scholar, I.I.T., New Delhi and Dr. Ravindra Kumar, now in University Grant Commission, New Delhi, who extended their cooperation to facilitate completion of this research work.

I will be failing my duties if I do not express my gratitude to Dr. S.P. Jain, Regional Director, NIPCCD, Regional Centre, Lucknow, for having extended cooperation in permitting leave to complete my work.

My special thank goes to Shri B.K. Bhattacharjee of NIPCCD, Regional Centre, Lucknow, who has made painstaking efforts in typing the manuscript. I am also thankful to Shri B.S. Nagi, Sr. Research Associate, CDS, New Delhi, who helped in data analysis on computer.

SALIL KUMAR.

[illegible] guidance [illegible] [illegible] [illegible] [illegible] Dr. [illegible] [illegible] [illegible] [illegible] [illegible] [illegible] [illegible] [illegible] [illegible] [illegible] [illegible] suggestion to facilitate [illegible] [illegible]

[illegible] [illegible] [illegible] Dr. [illegible] [illegible] [illegible] [illegible] complete my work.

[illegible] [illegible] [illegible] [illegible] [illegible] [illegible] [illegible]

[illegible]

SECTION I

1

INTRODUCTION

In the present day context an endeavour in every area is witnessed for Development in the country. Development implies the existence of a goal and a progress towards the goal. Human resource is one of the most vital resources of a country as it exploits the natural environment for the entire population. Thus, all the aspects of development—scientific and technological, economic and social to name a few—can be evaluated on the criterion of their utility and service for the welfare of human being. All aspects of Development are, therefore, aids to Human Development. The development of an individual in an organization would imply that we discover what his potentialities are and give him / her adequate opportunities to develop those potentials, which, of course, would be useful to the organization also. It is in fact, the manpower, or in other words, human resource which constitutes an organization and makes it grow and develop. Hence, Human Resource Development (HRD) approach has gained wide acceptance. HRD, in the organizational context, is viewed as a process by which employees of an organization are continuously helped in a planned way to acquire capabilities (knowledge, perspectives, attitudes and skills) required to perform various tasks or functions associated with their present or future expected roles, to develop their general enabling capabilities as individuals so that they are able to discover and utilize their own potential for their own organization development, and to develop an organizational culture where superior-subordinate relationships, team work and collaboration among different sub-units are strong and contribute to the organizational health, dynamism and pride of employees. The growth and development of employees depends upon the organization's policies and strategies for Organizational Development (OD). In the OD approach systematic attempts are made to bring about desirable changes in job-designs, enrichment of jobs at the organizational level to make the job-tasks more interesting and meaningful and at the individual level enhancement in knowledge, skill, perspectives and job attitudes are brought about through the process of training which crucially contributes to achieve the goal of HRD in the organization. Thus, training is considered a major means of OD and important strategy for HRD. The HRD and OD approaches have been used for organizational growth and development through training. Simultaneously, efforts for optimizing industrial productivity are substantiated by introducing technological innovations intended to minimize costs and efforts. Different technologies and processes become costly and obsolete with each scientific and technological innovation being introduced in an industrial organization. With the expanding organizational growth an urgent need is felt for management development. Management development is considered one of the most important areas of management of the human resources which, in turn, leads to organizational development. The underlying assumption is that the success of an organization to a great extent depends on the quality of its managers. Development of managers, therefore, has been considered a crucial aspect of organizational strategies including the job enrichment opportunities for managers. At the psychological level training programmes contribute to managerial growth, confidence, effectiveness and personal adjustment needed to be better adjusted with the job requirements and also with the organizational climate. Training, on the other hand, compete with changing demands and there is a constant need to develop continuing education and training programmes which equip personnel to understand new concepts and apply technological innovations in an organization. Providing equal opportunities of growth to personnel by the organization is another way of looking at the phenomenon keeping in view the HRD perspective. Scientific and technological advances have brought in a variety of changes in the lifestyle and working patterns of individual and attitudinal changes have been witnessed in the past few decades. These changes in attitudes and thinking have also led to change in different roles and jobs. Resultantly equal job opportunities are now being offered to both males and females. There are many new jobs that are offered to applicants. New entrants selected for a job need to be trained. Increasing population also produces demand for training as in future more and more individuals would be selected and will require to be trained by the organization. In recent years it has been realised that a humanistic perspective providing growth opportunities to employees is important and need to be considered as a philosophy of training.

Different training techniques have been used by organizations to equip their employees with due consideration to their existing knowledge, skills and training techniques intended to bring about changes in attitudes so that appropriate job attitudes are developed. Training situation facilitates learning and increases motivation of the individual. One of the essential conditions for learning process is that the individual should be motivated to learn. Thus learning and motivation are pre-requisites for any type of training. Training process is likely to be less effective and useful for an individual participant and his organization if the individual is not willing to learn. Learning takes place on the foundation of existing behaviour which a trainee brings to the learning situation. There are individual differences in this respect. Almost in all types of training programmes trainees constitute a heterogeneous group with different levels of their educational background, personality and varied socio-economic backgrounds. An effective training programme must carefully evaluate the personal and psychological factors that affect the individual trainee in the training situation. Probably the design of training module can be determined by the type of trainees. The motivational possibilities that a trainee brings to the training situation as a result of his past experiences and personality leading to particular type of his perception of the training situation are important correlates of management training programmes and other on-the job training programmes. However, in the process of designing management development programmes the characteristics of the manager participants have not been given due consideration.

There are different approaches to analyse the training programmes. Management Development (MD) training programmes have also been discussed as the job-enrichment strategies for the organization leading to the Organizational Development (OD). Issues related to OD also emphasize on client's motivation to change as an important implementation strategy. According to Parmeswaran (1983) different psychological approaches to behaviour have led to appreciate the importance of MD training programmes. These approaches suggest that individual differences should not be overlooked. As mentioned above, learning, perception and motivation are basic and independent processes, nevertheless they are interrelated and are influenced by one another. Effective learning depends on adequate motivation. Many motives are the result of learning. Personal growth depends both on motivation and learning, further both learning and motivation are influenced by attitude which are also influenced by motivation and learning, thus forming a close cycle on inter-relatedness. However, effective performance depends on the interplay of perception, learning, motivation and personal growth. The emphasis on overall development of personality of trainees is the objective of most of the training programmes today. The contemporary MD programmes aim at developing effective human beings who are effective managers. A well conceived MD programme, therefore, has to be aware of the generality of behavioural characteristics. The MD programmes thus planned have been considered successful in achieving the objective of optimum HRD in organizations.

Manager secures results through people but he does so by performing a special kind of work of which human relations is only a part. Organizationally the manager is removed from the immediate responsibilities of those he supervises. Thus he is the only man who can view the individual needs of his subordinates with objectivity, perspective and balance. Further, because he is a member of a group of supervisors who, in turn, report to a common superior at the higher level, he is in a position to interpret and reconcile the needs of supervisors and the organization as a whole (Merril and Marting, 1970). Hence need for Management Development training programme to achieve the goals of optimum HRD and OD.

In the light of the above, it is evident that managers are the key personnel who secure results in fulfilment of the needs of the organization as a whole. All training efforts are, therefore, focussed on developing an effective manager in the ideal sense, but individuals are, from their very nature, people first, showing different characteristics of temperament. Moreover, it is a variety of the personality which makes the most effective team. In other words, individual differences have an important role in a team of personnel to be an effective team in job performance. Any attempt to MD, therefore, needs to be focussed on growth and development of managers keeping in view their personal characteristics and psychological factors effecting them which, in turn, would also facilitate employee growth and development in the organization.

Studies show that a number of other personal characteristics may influence the impact of job enrichment on employee reactions. Stone (1977-79) reported that individuals often perceive the same sensory stimulus in different ways, their perception of the objective characteristics of a particular job may be influenced by several factors. The perception of identical tasks vary from one individual to another as a function of age, education, job tenure, and field independence. These findings clearly indicate that organizations must manage not only the actual design of jobs but also the processes by which jobs are perceived. Thus, personality variables influence job-enrichment programmes for job design. Closely linked with job-enrichment is the concept of Quality of Work Life (QWL).

In the aforesaid context the present study is planned to find out relationship between some psychological variables and training experience. The investigation emphasizes a humanistic-cognitive approach to analyse and offer bases for meaningful and useful plan for management development programmes. The study has been planned to study the impact of some personality and work related factors on training experience of managers who received training in two different types of organizations. The study makes a contribution in designing meaningful, effective and need-based training modules for Management Development Training Programmes. The following chapter deals with concept and trends of MD training, model of the study, models of MD, and earlier studies in training and MD and theoretical orientations to training and learning.

2

MANAGEMENT DEVELOPMENT TRAINING APPROACHES

In recent times different training techniques have been used by organizations to equip their employees with knowledge, skills, attitudes for employees' personal growth and development leading to development of the organization. Efforts have been made to design and develop different types of management training/ management education programmes leading to management development.

Training has been differentiated from education by educationists. Training refers to the teaching of a specific skill. Training is structured and stratified and can be communicated objectively by one person to another. Education, on the other hand, refers to imparting of knowledge which is contextual and serves as a necessary 'floor' for understanding and practising skills. Education may or may not have the sharp vocational focus which the training necessarily has.

The term development has been defined as the process which not only inculcates skills — vocational and non-specific, but also encourages and improves the ability to teach and train oneself and others. It aims at the development of individual's whole personality. It is essentially a process to create the capacity to grow and allow others as well to grow.

Thus, development is aimed through the process of training. With the changing times emphasis on training is ever-increasing and training has been viewed as essential for HRD and OD. The demand for trained and skilled personnel is on the increase with expanding industrial organizations and development of organizations, not only in private sector but also in the public sector, which has gained manifold impetus in India. With the development process need for training is felt all the more and training has been considered an important activity for optimum Human Resource Development (HRD) and Organizational Development (OD). So much—so that presently lot of emphasis is placed on training in the Government departments and organizations with a view to enhance the job skills and professional development of officials, managers and those who supervise employees.

Classroom training is considered less useful for skill and competence development of the employees in industrial settings. The goals of development of skills and competence through training resulted in planning and designing of job-oriented and specific training programmes, especially in the past two decades. These training programmes have been designed to meet the training requirements of personnel working at different levels in an organization. Management training aims at developing highly specific and immediately useful skills. Management training is intended to prepare managers to carry out well-known tasks in well-defined job contexts. deBettings (1925) has explained that MD encompasses the whole—a complex process by which managers as individuals learn, grow and improve their abilities to perform management tasks in a professional way. The success or failure of an organization depends largely on the quality of management. The quality of management may be improved by imparting training to managers, thereby offering opportunities for growth and development.

The objectives of Management Development (MD) training programmes, thus, are to maximise managerial effectiveness and personal adjustment, growth and development of trainees. The MD training programmes at the same time aim at optimizing human resource development in organizations. The basic assumption in all the MD training programmes is that in an ideal situation, managerial effectiveness, and personal adjustment and growth are inseparable and both facilitate each other mutually. A MD training programme must have these two objectives of performance for a short time overlooking these factors, but in the long run, it is impossible and will lead to consequences which will affect the productivity. In addition, serious problems of dissatisfaction, employees turnover, irresponsibility may also arise. The current approach of person-centredness is based on a number of psychological assumptions, which, in turn, lead to the approach of optimizing the HRD.

The MD programmes have produced functional specialists instead of managers. In the sixties, this view had been put forward by many management practitioners, academicians and researchers. Andrews (1957, a, b), Anshen (1955), Argyris (1955, 56), Bach (1951) are some to name a few. Similar situation existed contemporarily in India too. The pattern of MD training in the sixties had been reviewed by these researchers and it was pointed out that many MD programmes were not producing the expected results. Two basic reasons for this were attributed: (a) failure to identify what a manager must do in managing and to develop and train managers to do this kind of work, and (b) the assumption that managers could be trained to manage away from the job. Courses, seminars and conferences are indispensable part of the training process but they can fill up only gaps in knowledge and provide a certain amount of practice in management techniques. According to this view, the managers can learn only through direct application of managerial knowledge and skills to the responsibilities of their jobs. This called for a review of the objectives of the MD training programmes and off-the-job training had been replaced by on-the-job training. Nevertheless, off-the-job training has not lost its usefulness, and importance in MD. Moreover, emphasis from development of merely skills and effectiveness of managers on their job tasks has been shifted to the integrated development of the management personnel, keeping in view of the basic needs of individuals for training and personal growth and development.

Training process is likely to be less effective and useful for an individual and organization if the individual is not willing to learn.

Learning takes place on the foundation of existing behaviour which a trainee brings to the learning situation. There are individual differences in this respect. Almost in all types of training programmes trainees constitute a heterogeneous group with different levels of educational background, different personality and different socio-economic background. An effective training programme must carefully evaluate the individual differences in trainees. Perhaps the design of the training module can be determined by the type of trainees after determining needs for training. The motivational possibilities that a trainee brings to the training situation is a result of his past experience and personality leading to his perception of training experience are important correlates of management development training. Thus MD not only includes the processes by which managers and executives require various skills and competence in their present jobs, but also capacities for future management tasks of increasing difficulty and scope.

Thus, Management Development training refers to the process of educating and developing employees so that they have the knowledge, skills and attitudes, and understanding needed to manage in future.

MODEL OF THE STUDY AND MODELS OF MANAGEMENT DEVELOPMENT

The management development process has been viewed in terms of different models that usually emphasize either one particular aspect or approach to management. The model proposed in this study is based on various theoretical orientations with specific reference to cognitive and intrinsic factors influencing the training experience. The present study emphasizes training experience as a job-enrichment strategy which can be explained through the humanistic-organismic approach emphasizing the need to grow as the basic motivational factor. How the individual trainee perceives the training programme is important to understand the psychological correlates of training attitudes. The factors included in the study are depicted in the model given on the following page.

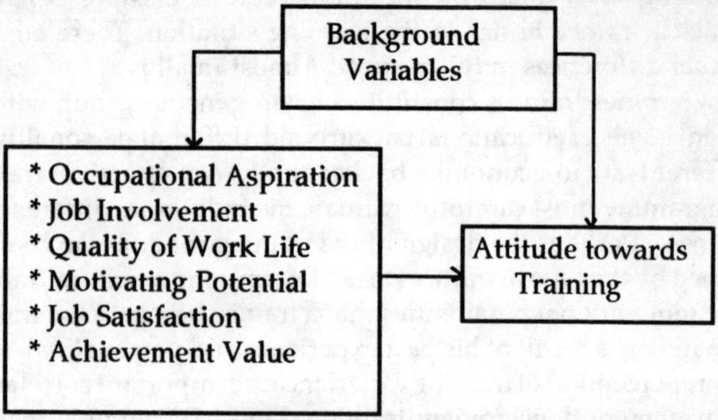

The management process has been viewed in terms of different models that usually emphasize either one particular aspect or approach to management. It would be appropriate to have an overview of different models which explain management development process.

Administration Model

The basic model, which is composed of the basic management functions viz., planning, organizing, directing, controlling, coordinating and evaluating, is referred to as an administration model. The model was proposed by Doraiswami (1983) which comprises these functions with a few refinements made in the concept of administration. These refinements are: (i) environmental scanning is an added input, (ii) objective formulation is specifically emphasized, (iii) the main purpose of direction has been clarified in the model as control and coordination, and (iv) a feedback loop is introduced connecting evaluation with the other components of the model which is necessary in management process. The model is somewhat simplistic and descriptive rather than conceptual or fundamental because of tremendous development of management theory, in recent past. The model although not faulty fails to hint at anything which could be identified as "core" of the management process.

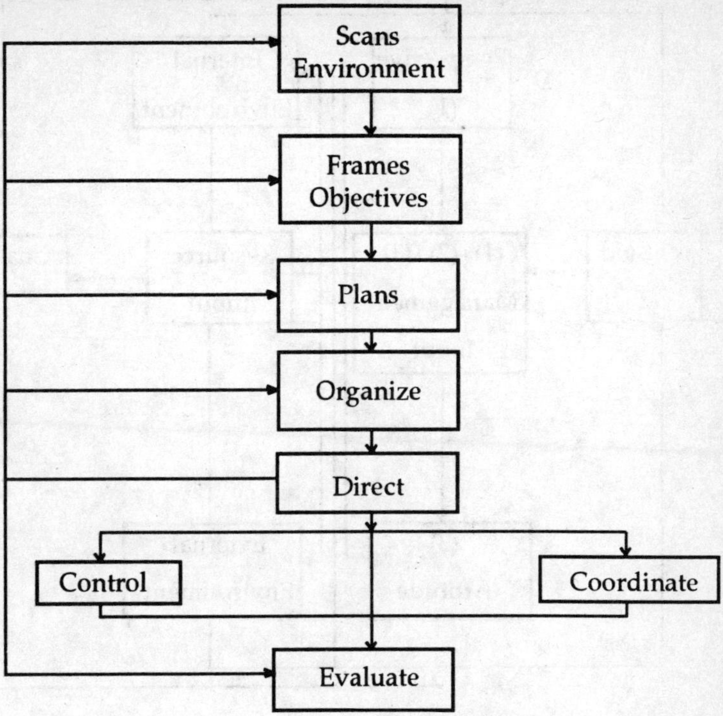

Model 1 : *Administration Model*

Synthesizing Model

An improvement in the administration model of simple functional sequence has been made in synthesizing model. The synthesizing model has viewed the management development as essentially a synthesizing activity which involves synthesis at two levels. A management input package is synthesized from three separate inputs: perspective, methods and attitudes. Raw-material input package is similarly synthesized from the separate inputs: environment (internal and external) and resources (man, material and money). The managerial and the raw-material input packages react with each other to produce an output package which is referred to in the model as goals. The feedback loops in the model indicate inter-connections and circular causations.

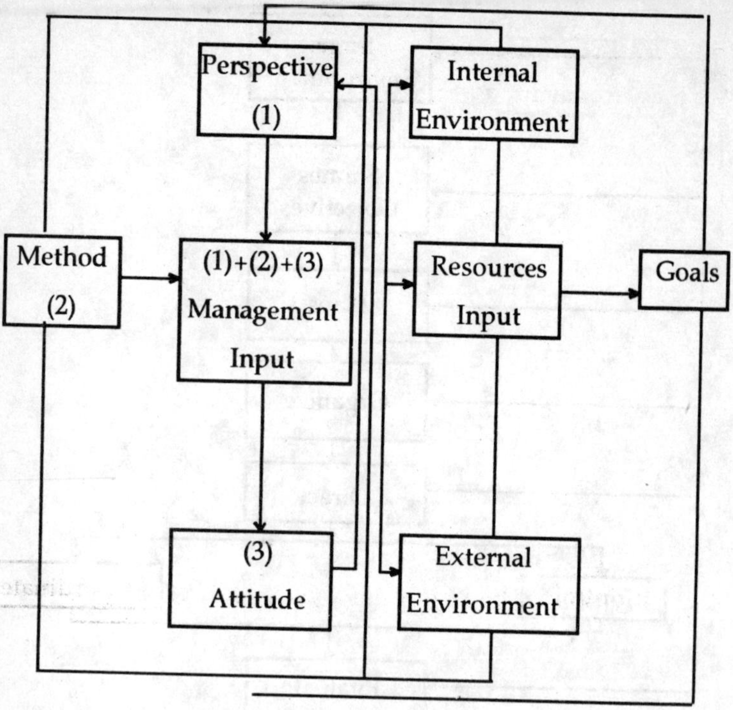

Model 2: *Synthesizing Model*

Features added in this model are the following: (i) the concept of distinctive managerial input has been termed as influencing output, (ii) the influence of external and internal environment is shown on resource conversion, (iii) the concept of synthesis of component inputs has been used as distinctly from their mere combined use, and (iv) the personal element in management is typified by perspective and attitudes unlike earlier models impersonal presentation of various functions.

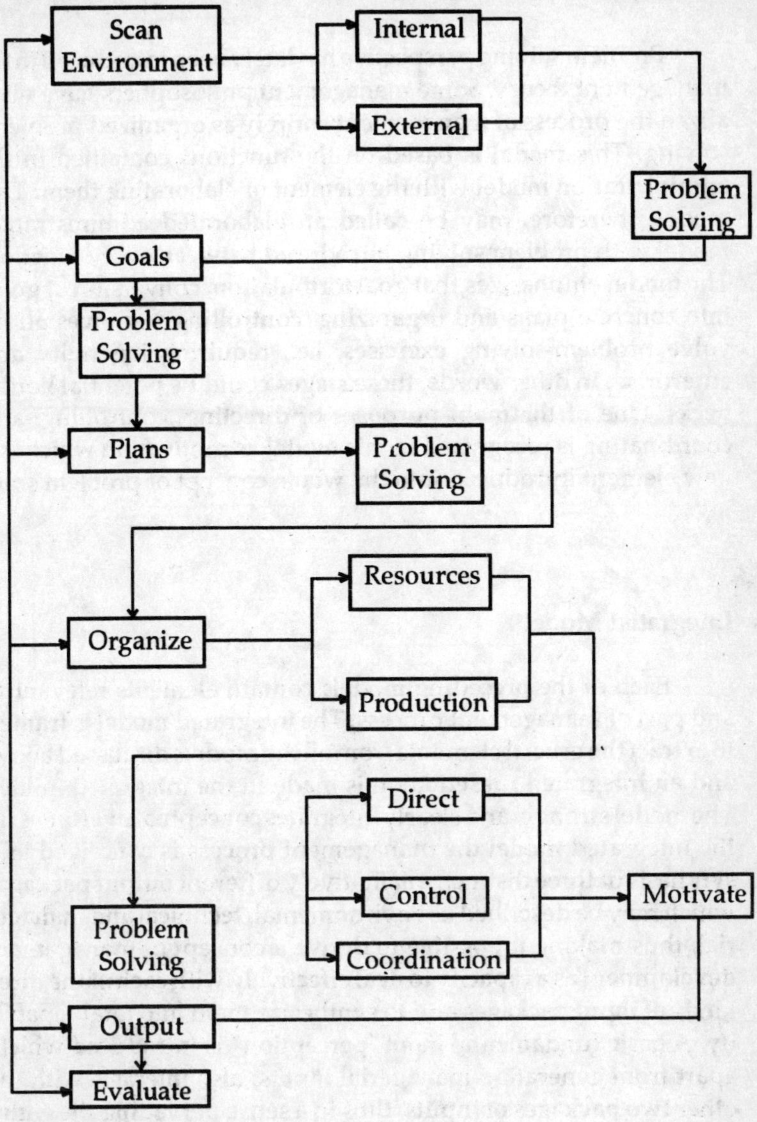

Model 3: *Problem-solving Model*

Problem-solving Model

Problem solving perspective has lately been introduced in the management theory. Some management philosophers have visualized the process of management entirely as organized problem-solving. This model is based on the functions contained in the administration model with the element of elaborating them. This model, therefore, may be called an elaborated administration model with problem solving introduced between every function. The model emphasizes that goal formulation, conversion of goals into concrete plans and organizing/controlling resources all involve problem-solving exercises, i.e., requiring ingenuity and enterprise. In other words, these stages could be potential bottlenecks. One of the main purposes of directing, controlling, and coordinating is recognised in this model as motivation which is a new element introduced into the whole concept of problem solving.

Integrated Model

Each of the preceding models contain elements relevant to and part of management process. The integrated model is framed to extract the crucial elements from all the models discussed above and an integrated presentation is made in the integrated model. The model strongly and clearly integrates conceptual overtones. In the integrated model the management process is conceived as a synthesis of three distinct, qualitatively different output packages which may be described as environmental, technical and managerial, thus making it possible to derive a concept of management development as a capacity to deal effectively with each of the three kinds of input packages and to synthesize them into total capability. A basic fundamental input "perception" is introduced which, apart from generating managerial inputs, also interacts with the other two packages of inputs, thus in a sense pervading the entire process. Scanning abstracts from the environment not only customer's needs which should be profitably exploited by the organization for its own benefit but also other factors which could include socially relevant factors like population, occupational hazards, etc., thus widening the social basis of marketing goals.

The internal and external environment affects all the functional inputs. Within the general input of problem solving a specific component "innovation" is introduced in the model which could cover in day-to-day, familiar areas as well as original research and development efforts, thus expanding the intellectual horizon of the management process. The main thrust of the integrated model may be simplified and summarized in the following way:

(i) Manager's perception of (a) the environment; (b) his own problem-solving capability, and (c) technical capability jointly lead to goal formulation.

(ii) Clearly formulated goals together with the above two types of capabilities lead to the identification, organization, and control of necessary resources and their conversion into output.

(iii) Evaluation of the output reinforces or modified perception and starts the cycle all over again.

(iv) Problem solving and technical capabilities are useful in perceiving and influencing the environment to some extent.

In addition to the five models described above, Gilmer and Deci (1971) have also proposed a model. They have considered training as a process of training development and implementation and have proposed a training-development system. In development of training materials the model suggests activities that a training specialist would perform. In this model Phase 1 is job study in which task analysis, job description and job design would be analyzed. In Phase 2 training objectives would be identified based on job study. Phase 3 of activities would be to develop criterion measure which would be decided by input measures of entering behaviour of trainees and output measures of course mastery and effective job performance after training. In Phase 4 instructional procedure would be selected keeping in view instructional strategies and motivation of trainees and finally Phase 5 target and revision cycles would follow. Information for Phase 1 to 5 would be obtained from feedback which the expert would get from tryouts of the training course. Phase 6 would serve as feedback to restart the whole process.

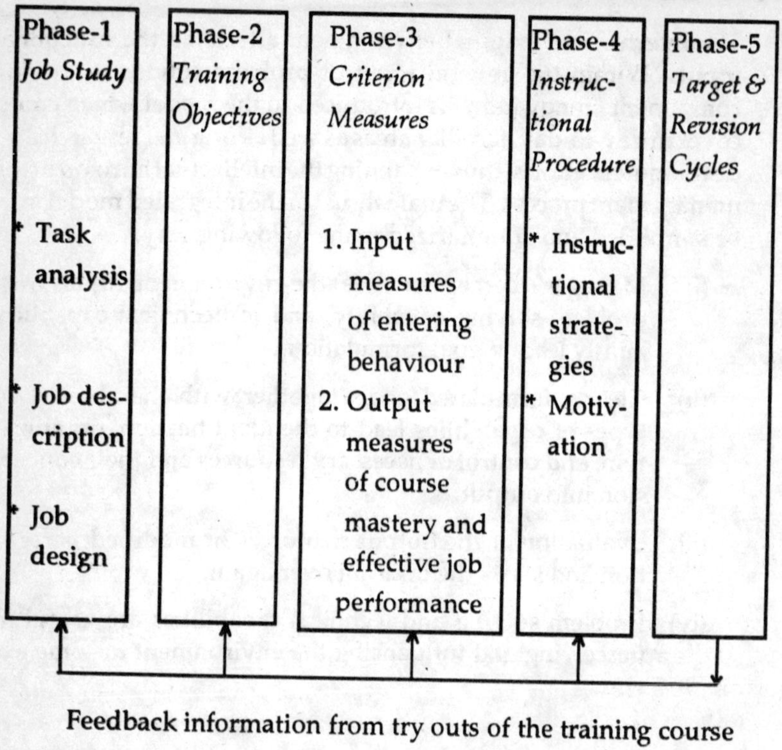

Model 6: *The Phases of a training development system showing the activities that a training specialist would perform in development training materials.*

The models for management development process and MD training reviewed above lack consideration for the psychological factors and individual differences factor. These models therefore need adding some psychological and individual different factors for a better understanding of the MD programmes. Training programmes for MD have also been suggested as job enrichment strategies which are outcome of the Herzberg et al (1959) two factor model of motivation.

Theoretical Approaches

A number of theories have been given to explain human

motivation to work. One such controversial yet popular theory of work motivation was based on study conducted by Herzberg et al (1959). They conducted a motivational study and concluded that job satisfiers were labelled as motivators and dissatisfiers were called hygiene factors. The motivators refer to Herzberg's job enrichment theory of motivation. According to the theory an individual must have a job with a challenging content, development and growth, opportunities, variety, etc., in order to be truly motivated. Herzberg drew attention to the importance of job-content factors in work motivation which previously had been badly neglected and often totally overlooked. The practical motivation technique of job enrichment is also one of the significant contribution of Herzberg et al (1959).

Job enrichment has provided probably the greatest impetus for job design. Job enrichment approach focussed on providing opportunities for employee growth through vertical job loading which introduced a greater depth of responsibility.

Case studies of job enrichment applications have also shown that the approach has potential and the job enrichment model has provided thrust for recent job design approach. However, the problem of individual differences needs further attention.

Job Characteristics Approach

The job characteristics study was carried out by Turner and Lawrence (1965). Six attributes related to work attitudes and to a lesser extent worker attendance were: (a) variety, (b) autonomy, (c) required interaction, (d) optional interaction, (e) knowledge, and skill required, and (f) responsibility. These six characteristics are fairly consistent with combined set of job factors which have been used by job enrichment perspectives. Worker values are important factors that have role in job enrichment for the job design.

Hackman and Lawler (1971) identified four core job characteristics —variety, autonomy, task identify, and feed-back—and two less critical characteristics. They developed a measure of higher-order that need strength.

Hackman and Oldham (1975) have developed the Job Diagnostic Survey, a measure of job characteristics and the Growth Need Strength Scale, a scale for measuring individual characteristics. Growth Need Strength is the degree to which a person desires complex, challenging work. The core job characteristics combine to influence critical psychological states, experienced meaningfulness of the work and knowledge of the actual results of work activities.

Effect of Individual Characteristics on Job Enrichment

Besides person's Growth-Need Strength (GNS), a number of other personal characteristics may influence the impact of job enrichment on employee reactions. Stone (1977, 1979) mentioned that individuals often perceive the same sensory stimulus in different ways their perception of the objective characteristics of a particular job may be influenced by several factors. The perception of identical tasks varies significantly from one individual to another as a function of age, education, job tenure, cognitive structure of the individual, dominance, and field independence. These findings clearly indicate that organizations must manage not only the actual design of jobs but also the processes by which jobs are perceived. Thus, the personality variables which influence the job enrichment programmes for job design need further attention.

Quality of Work Life

Closely linked with job enrichment is the concept of Quality of Work Life (QWL). The QWL has been defined as the degree to which members of a work organization are able to satisfy important personal needs through their experiences in the organizations. The definition implies the QWL can be assured by measures of need importance and need satisfaction.

The QWL refers to the interaction between individual employees and their organization. The need for material rewards and changes to learn and grow must somehow be meshed with the needs of the organization, for attaining goal of productivity, creativity, reliability, loyalty and high performance. Job enrichment may be the part of the diverse changes that might be thought to be brought in order to achieve the goal of increasing QWL.

The QWL is also related to the needs of individuals. There is, therefore, necessity to apply needs analysis to gain knowledge about individuals and organizational needs so that both may be meshed together for growth and development of employees as well as organization. Brinkerhoff (1986) has emphasized on expanding needs analysis by redefining the function of needs analysis to realise organization goals.

Magar and Pipe (1970) and Rummler (1976) have mentioned that in order to avoid providing training to meet non-training problems, needs-analysis has been constructed as a "problem solving" effort.

It is necessary to recognize the value component of need for expanded understanding of needs analysis. When it is said that something is needed means that is necessary or useful in serving some valued purpose e.g., money by itself meets no need but has utility in gaining things that are valued. Similarly, training by itself provides no outcome that has intrinsic value. The value of training outcomes may be established only relative to the degree that they serve, or are useful for achieving something that the organization values. Thus, needs analysis must establish the potential value of training efforts to the organization, and needs analysis must also answer basic questions: (a) What good, if any, can training do? and (b) How valuable, relative to other possible, "goals", is the "good" that training can do?

Needs analysis closely relates to evaluation. Stufflebeam (1977) reviewed many examples of needs analysis in various fields and identified four useful definitions of needs. Each definition fits different training situations, leads to different training value bases and implies the use of different needs analysis methods, viz., discrepancy, democratic, diagnostic, and analytic. Discrepancy is defined as a difference between an ideal normative or expected level of performance and an actual level of performance. By comparison needs may be identified.

A democratic need is the preference by the majority. People

may not be aware of what someone else believes about their needs. Participation in the needs definition process generates commitment and acceptance, and can enhance performance in later training.

Diagnostic needs are defined through research and casual analysis. HRD should concern itself with what is right in an organization as well as what is wrong.

Analytic needs are discovered by intuition, insight, expert consideration, and enlightenment.

Use of systems to describe and develop human resources has been used during the past few years. Systems provide a logical and thorough approach. In human resource development, systems-method has been utilized in the design of instructional systems so as to meet the need of groups. Use of systems approach would facilitate to find out specific objectives of a training programme.

Learning Theories and Management Development Programmes

The educationists have differentiated education and training by stating that training is narrow in scope and involves only learning that is related to job performance, while education is concerned with the total human being and his insights into and understanding of his entire world.

Learning means the following for training:

(a) Knowing something intellectually or conceptually a trainee never knew before.

(b) Being able to do something the trainee could not do before—behaviour or skill.

(c) Combining two knowledges into a new understanding of a skill, piece of knowledge, concept, or behaviour.

(d) Being able to understand and/or apply that which a trainee knows—either knowledge, or behaviour.

The learning theories may be categorized into five schools of learning according to This and Lippitt (1971):, (a) Behaviour School, (b) Gestalt School, (c) Functionalist School, (d) Mathematical School, and (e) Current Learning Schools.

(a) The Behaviourist School

These theories hold that learning results from the reward or punishment that follows a response to a stimulus. These theories are also known as S-R (Stimulus - Response) Theories.

(b) Gestalt School

Gestalt theorists believe that learning is not as simple as a stimulus-response connection. They are of the view that learning is a cognitive process and involves the whole personality of the learner. To the Gestalt theorists, learning is infinitely more complex than what the S-R theories would indicate. To them learning may occur even simply by thinking about a problem. Kurt Lewin, Wolfgang Kohler, E.C. Talman and Max Wertheimer are the prominent theorists of Gestalt School.

(c) Functionalist School

The Functionalists have agreed with almost all the theories of learning. They view learning as a complex phenomenon which is not explained by the Gestalt or Behavioural theories adequately.

(d) Mathematical School

The researchers that represent Mathematical School of Theories are of the view that learning must be stated in mathematical form. These theorists belong to different learning schools but they tend to focus on mathematical models such as the Feed-back Model, Information-Theory Model, Gaming Model, Differential Calculus Model, Stochastic Model, and Statistical Association Model. These theories, however, do not represent a theory, but have attempted to explain the research findings of other theories in mathematical terms.

(e) Current Learning Theory Schools

The current approach to learning takes its threads from Gestalt and Behavioural Theories and with modifications in both types of theories, some researchers have tried to accommodate two pieces of both the schools of learning. Their assumption is that training involves the whole man, i.e., psychological, physiological, biological and neuro-physiological. Some of these are the postulates of MacCorquodale and Mehl and the Social learning theory of Rotter (Lippitt, This and Bidwell, Jr., 1971).

Adult Learner

Management Training has to invariably take into account the characteristics of an adult learner. The basic characteristics of adult learner are the following:

(a) The average adult learner intellectually, and otherwise performs as well, as an average younger participant and the trainer himself.

(b) Adults, who actively and continuously participate and are involved in the training programme, learn more effectively. Learning skills require practice to be maintained.

(c) Adults learn more effectively when they are permitted to learn at their own pace.

Learning theories closely relate to MD training, as development of specific skills requires knowledge of the learning theories. Knowledge of learning theories facilitates design of specific training modules for development of specific skills in MD training. However, more than one theory of learning may be utilized to meet out the specific training requirements..

Harris and Fleishman (1955) designed a research study to evaluate the effect of human relations supervisory training programme in terms of the attitudes and behaviours of the trainees after they had returned for the actual work situations. It was one of the first such studies to follow up the effects of supervisory training. The previous researches had usually followed the procedure of evaluating the training immediately upon completion of the training programme. Supervisory behaviour was evaluated by Harris and Fleishman (1955) in terms of two criteria of performance (the ratings of the supervisors by those who worked under them served as dependent variable). The two scores obtained from questionnaires was Initiating Structure and Consideration. At least three workers were drawn randomly from each of the work groups of 98 different foremen at two time periods 11 months apart. During the 11 months interval between the two evaluations, 39 foremen had attended the company's central school which administered the Supervisory Training Programme. The remaining 59 had received no human relation training during the same period. No significant differences were found in the mean scores made by either group before and after the training period. Also no significant changes in mean scores occurred within/either group, whether or not they had received supervisory training. Harris and Fleishman (1955) also found much the same sort of non-effect when they examined the influence of a refresher course upon supervisory behaviour. The effects of human relations training may also be temporary at the best, and exceeding care should therefore be taken before investing greatly in such a training programme.

The field of MD training in India in the recent years has developed rapidly, and training procedures and practices have been increasingly adopted by more and more organizations including the public sector organizations. Another aspect of development of training programme is increasing diversity in the training programmes which caters essentially to different kinds and levels of managerial personnel. Vertical growth of MD training programmes is evident by the current practice of extending the training to the top level of managerial personnel.

Psychological Theories of MD Training

The Management Development training has been influenced by theories and practices of behavioural scientists. Radical changes have been brought in the training and development of new types of training programmes with new objectives. In the recent training modules training techniques such as sensitivity training and training of personal growth and development are used. Management training tries to shape the person rather than his performance. It aims at long term productivity to immediate production goals. It also looks at the individuals as long term asset and investment. This change in outlook is attributed to the attitudinal differences among individuals. MD training, therefore is a field of activity where the impact of psychological approaches has been marked.

Parmeswaran (1983) has stressed that different psychological approaches to human behaviour are important to MD training. The different psychological approaches are—Psychodynamic approach (which emphasizes the role of motivational factors in human behaviour), the Humanistic Organismic Approach (which emphasizes on the hierarchy of needs of motives and the need to grow as a basic motivational factor), the Behavioural Approach (places emphasis on reward and punishment), Stimulus-Response relationship, and the Cognitive Approach (which stresses upon the perception of the individual).

The Cognitive Approach is phenomenological and derives its support from the work of German psychologists Wertheimer, Koffka, and Kohler known as Gestalt Psychologists. This approach emphasizes the role of perceptual factors in behaviour. According to this approach the behaviour of an individual is primarily determined by the way in which he looks at or interprets a situation. Thus, perception of an individual have bearing on the performance, organizational situations and factors. The Cognitive Approach depends on the adequacy and meaningfulness of the perception. Thus, in many management development training programmes emphasis is on developing the right type of perceptions and right kind of attitudes from perceptions. In the sensitivity training programmes emphasis is on the role of perceptions which include perception of oneself and perception of others.

Many problems in organizations arise from lack of sensitivity to others' and own genuine problems. These training programmes are, therefore, designed to enable the individuals to develop right type of perceptions which, in turn, lead to desired attitudes. The MD training especially designed for management personnel must primarily concentrate on this aspect.

Different approaches to behaviour have suggested that there is inter-dependence of learning, perception, motivation and psychological growth which are influenced by one another. Thus, effective learning depends on adequate motivation. Many motives are the result of learning and personal growth depends on motivation and learning. Both learning and motivation are influenced by perception which is also influenced by motivation and learning. This interplay of these independent psychological processes is important if learning is to take place and therefore these cannot be overlooked in Management Development training programmes.

Besides the approaches and theories, a review of earlier researches in training and Management Development would not be out of place. The following chapter deals with the earlier studies in training and MD.

3

EARLIER STUDIES IN TRAINING AND MANAGEMENT DEVELOPMENT

Huge volumes of research in the area are available which may be classified into six types of studies: researches on training, management development, models and theories, organizational development, job design and job aids and studies in India.

Singh (1986) has mentioned that almost all large corporations have formal training programmes and in many corporate sectors training budgets are comparable to the budgets of many large Universities in U.S.A. In India many large organizations in public and private sectors have their training departments conducting training programmes on the basis of the identified needs. Their dependence on outside courses is limited. Mostly 'in-house' training programmes are conducted by these training departments in organizations.

The situation in the Government departments is contrary to that in the public and private sectors. However, a few State Governments have their own Management Development Training Institute. There are autonomous training institutes functioning under the Ministries of the Government of India that are assigned the responsibility of training of Government officials and functionaries of developmental programmes and schemes.

An overview of researches by Campbell et al (1970) enlists 22 distinct training methods which are applicable to MD. House (1967), Blum and Naylor (1968), Lynton and Pareek (1967), have also enlisted different types of training methods. Foreman (1967), Quakenboss (1969), Utgaard and Davis (1970) considered the frequency with which various training techniques were used. On-the-job training, job rotation, lectures, conference and seminar methods are used by majority of organizations (i.e., 75% to 90%) while techniques such as simulation, role playing, programmed instructions and T-groups are used by a relatively smaller number of organizations (15% to 20%). A wide range of researches in training include basic encounter and personal growth training, television and telephone training, cross-cultural training, programmes and computer assisted instruction, orientation training, sales training, team training, simulation and speciality programmes.

Basic Encounter and Personal Growth Training

There was an increasing emphasis on the T-group training researches for even more existential and less intellectual group experiences, as it was evident from Buchanan and Schindler-Rainman (1969) who described the personal growth experience. The personal growth training has been emphasized in an attempt to develop overall personality of the managers so as to be a successful person and a successful manager at the same time. Personal growth training emphasizes on learning about one's self through a loosely planned sequence of physical activities. These experiences are usually designed to promote a loosening and expression of feelings and emotions.

Television and Telephone Training

Video tape has been a widely used technique for training. It has been used as a feedback mechanism. Kennedy (1970) suggested how video can be used in training the 'hardcore', and Stoller (1968) described examples in sensitivity training and group counselling. The review of Training Magazine and Training and Development Journal reveals that video has been widely used for different types of training programmes and the telephone instructions have also been used for training in the USA.

Cross-Cultural Training

The 70's have experienced emphasis on training. Campbell (1969) summarised the type of programmes that have been used to train people for overseas assignments by the US military. Foster (1969) outlined a needs and task analysis for cross-cultural training. Lee (1968) outlined five problems encountered when developing managers in developing countries but he suggested no innovative solutions. A related study was conducted by Salas (1985) in Peru. Rodgers (1966) advocated an on-the-job training and counselling programme for developing foreign managers. Harrison and Hopkins (1967) described a living-in programme modelled after the NTL approach. Roberts (1970) reviewed cross-cultural studies which included training of managers also and found that the variable 'culture' was inadequately conceptualized. Roberts (1970) concluded that what was needed was to see research in systems terms and modern multivariate statistical procedures were needed to be adapted.

PROGRAMMED AND COMPUTER ASSISTED INSTRUCTION

Programmed Instruction (PI):

Most of the literature is concerned with one-time, one-place comparisons between a PI method and a conventional method using internal criteria as dependent variables. Herzberg, Steffen and Baxter (1965) compared a programmed text and a conventional text in teaching insurance fundamentals and demonstrated that the same could be covered in less time with PI. Subjects also preferred the PI method. Neidt and Meredity also found favourable attitudes towards PI than conventional texts in an Air Force technical course and the difference was greater for the high ability students. Mayo (1969) summarized a number of studies on PI conducted in the Navy and concluded that PI yielded similar learning in a shorter time than conventional methods, i.e., PI method was more efficient. Comparable achievements in a shorter time seems to be recurrent from PI research. However, there were two exceptions. Conor (1968) compared a teaching machine, PI text for a course in electrical engineering and found that both the teaching machine and PI text produced higher examination scores than the control group. Cavanagh and Jones (1968) compared a PI method to three conventional seminar methods for teaching management principles and found considerably higher scores for PI on a multiple choice criterion test.

Inconsistencies in the results of the above studies were explained by Pikas (1967); as shown by him, the criterion used to measure achievement may not be 'fair' to all methods, i.e., Brinkman (1966) compared PI to conventional method for teaching certain aspects of geometry. However, the criterion test was geared to the content of the PI mode which differed from the content of the conventional procedure. Mayo and Longo (1986) compared a 9-hour PI course to a 13-hour conventional course for teaching electronics fundamentals and found no differences on a test originally written for the conventional course but a significant difference on a test written on a test for the PI course. Rawls, Perry and Timmons (1966) carefully constructed a criterion test that favoured neither mode and found equal initial achievement but somewhat better retention and lower variability for the PI group. Long-term retention is largely a neglected research topic. The second possible explanation is that most of such comparative studies imply that PI is a conventional method, yet this variability in quality must surely be great within each of these two modes. Comparative studies are difficult because we have no quality control model for instructional strategies.

In the organizational setting external criteria are sometimes used to assess the effects of PI. Patten and Stermer (1969) used PI to train foremen in work standards but the results were equivocal. However, Cook (1967) used PI booklets to train regional saleswomen and the data suggested a significant increase in sales and lower turnover. A number of PI studies have focussed on certain parametric considerations. Individual differences, teaching machines vs programmed texts, the amount of material per frame, response mode (e.g., written vs oral), topic arrangement, pacing, and prompting vs confirmation or cueing vs knowledge of results (KR) are the major ones. The latter distinction refers to providing numerous cues or stimulus support before the response is made such that the correct response is always given vs reducing the probability of a correct response and providing post response KR. Two studies examined prompting vs confirmation. Seidel and Hunter (1968) found for a military technical speciality that stimulus support facilitates response acquisition during training but detracts from long term retention. Anderson, Faust and Roderick (1968) also show that heavy prompting hinders post-test performance. Variation is response mode (constructive response vs 'thinking it') had no significant effects. Berglund (1969) varied the degree of partial reinforcement or confirmation but found no significant difference on criterion test. Hartley (1968) has reviewed the PI literature on self vs external pacing. The conventional PI wisdom told that self pacing was the best but the data were not in complete agreement. A number of studies showed that external controls on the learner's pace had a facilitating effect. Noble (1969), and Cahoon, Paterson and Watson(1968) investigated that the interactions of various measures of individual differences with the achievement in PI and found no significant results, which is also a consistent finding in the literature. Johnson (1968) generated a number of programmes in which the topics were dispersed in varying degrees throughout the programme. Although the more dispersed programmes required more time; they led to better retention than when all the material on a topic was presented at a single location. Schuster (1968) tested a scrambled version which was compared to a linear branching version, but subjects much preferred the linear method. Several studies investigated three parameters at once. Welsh, Antoinetti and Thayer (1965) varied response mode, confirmation-no confirmation and the amount of review material in a PI course designed to teach insurance fundamentals. Attitudes and knowledge tests (varying in similarity to the programme itself) were the principal criteria. The review material helped slightly but response mode and confirmation made little difference. Also PI was only superior to the conventional method on the criterion test most similar to the programme. Whitlock (1967) varied pacing, number of frames and KR, and found no difference across treatment on a knowledge test. He also reported cogently that the better the basic programme, the less relevant are the parametric differences. Attwood and Wiener (1968, 1969) allowed subjects to select their own levels of KR, cueing and rate of stimulus presentation had beneficial effects. Additional reviews of PI studies have been given by Schramm (1964) and Burris (1968).

It may be concluded from above studies on PI that for appropriate material, PI is faster but probably does not lead to greater proficiency on an immediate post-test.

Computer Assisted Instruction (CAI)

A great deal of hardware and software has been constructed but the research efforts restricted largely to the area of elementary and secondary education, as reviewed by Campbell (1971). Two studies represented the research being conducted in organizations. For teaching data processing principles Schwarts and Haskell (1964) compared a PI text to a CAI system that incorporated more branches and skipped options. Achievement was the same but the CAI system was slightly faster. Using the similar CAI system Schwartz and Long (1967) could find few differences between CAI and a self study programme for teaching new developments in computer technology. Dick and Lotta (1969) compared CAI and PI in a student population and found PI to be slightly superior for teaching numerical concepts. The difference was due to the special difficulties that low ability students had with CAI.

Orientation Training

It seems obvious that an individual's initial period at work is extremely critical in terms of how he defines his activities, what he learns to expect from the organization and how he learns his job. Gomersall and Myers (1966) studied a one-day orientation programme for new production employees in a large electronics firm. The training was designed to reduce their anxiety by explaining what the company expected. The hazing they would probably get from experienced employees and the type of behaviour to expect from the supervisor. As compared to a control group, the trained group reached high production levels much more quickly. Lefkowitz (1970) experimented with different schedules for vestibule and on-the-job training for sewing machine operators. An initial day in the vestibule followed by a day on the line followed by more vestibule training seemed to have the most beneficial effects.

Sales Training

Harris and Vincent (1967) investigated the effects of a two-year life insurance training programme on 88 salesmen who were matched with 88 controls. Significant differences were found on first year premiums and size of policies produced. The investigators ruled out a self-selection explanation for the results but could not rule out the possibility of regression effects. Graves (1968) also studied life insurance sales training which included a three-day clinic in role playing interviews. Large differences were found in total sales and the six-month termination rate.

Training Through Television

Rawls and Rawls (1968) compared closed circuit television (CCTV) to conventional instruction in education psychology and discovered no differences in achievement or retention but found very negativistic attitude towards the TV mode. In addition students almost spent no time looking at the screen. Rock, Duva and Murray (1967) compared CCTV, films and conventional instruction in a military setting and demonstrated television to be at least as effective as the other modes.

Team Training

The Ohio State group studied two-man teams working in a

simulated radar situation where the objective was to track and intercept incoming aircraft. Johnston (1966) varied the amount of coordination and communication in the training task and demonstrated that team training was better than individual training when the criterion task required coordination between individuals. Naylor and Briggs (1965) investigated the effects of task complexity, task organization, and replacement of team members. They showed.that transfer of team skills varied with task complexity and that task organization was important only under the stress of changing team membership. The previous training experience of the replacement had only a very temporary effect on team performance. Briggs and Naylor (1965) used three-man teams and varied the degree of task organization and the fidelity of the training task (real radar scope vs a cardboard cut out). Team training did not transfer very well when the training simulation was of low fidelity. Briggs and Johnston (1966) studied this effect with regard to stimulus fidelity vs response fidelity and showed that stimulus fidelity was by far the most important. Klaus, Grant and Glaser (1967) used another laboratory task to examine the effects of different reinforcement patterns on team training and in the actual performance situation. Team reinforcement alone was not enough.

The studies cited above suggest that team training had value for transfer to tasks requiring inter-action, but the additional increment was quite fragile and could be largely obviated by lack of stimulus fidelity in the task or lack of individual reinforcement.

Simulation

Two studies dealt with fidelity problems in simulated training equipment. Hammerton and Tickner (1967) varied the fidelity of the remote operation of boy trolley. Background detail and depth cues during training were crucial for initial performance but training fidelity had few effects on long term retention and performance. Essentially the same finding was demonstrated in a study by Grimsley (1969) in which service personnel were trained on guided missile system controls of varying fidelity. Few differences in performances were observed when the criterion data were obtained four to six weeks after training. In management development a large number of simulation methods exist such as business games, case problems and role playing. Campbell et al (1970) pointed out that these methods seldom found their way into research studies and that their unique effects could be studied and they were most often combined with other techniques and the overall package would be 'evaluated'. The business game was infrequent exception. Rain (1966) demonstrated role playing in a business game improved test performance in a business policy course. Two levels of game complexity did not influence the results. Steinmetz and Patten (1967) showed only that students reacted favourably to using a business game in an accounting course.

Speciality Programmes

Chaney and Teel (1967) reported an excellent study of classroom instruction plus visual aids. A control group was compared to three experimental groups: classroom alone, visual aids alone and classroom combined by careful analysis of instructor performance and the criterion was the per cent of defects subsequently discovered on the job. The largest increment in the criterion resulted from using visual aids.

In one of the few cross-cultural studies conducted by Chembers (1969), he used the 'cultural assimilation' to train Americans in Iran. The technique asked the participants to analyze hypothetical situations in a specific culture and then provided feedback for right or wrong analysis. When asked to lead three-man Iranian problem-solving groups, the trained Americans were found to generate more favourable climate and better leader-member relations. However, group productivity did not change. Viteles (1969) reported a long term follow-up of executives who participated in the University of Pennsylvania's Humanistic Study Programme. The trends were towards more liberal attitudes and less emphasis on economic values, which were found in the original study, tended to hold up over the period of the follow-up.

Management Development (MD)

Campbell et al (1970) have summarized research on MD and

have reviewed 84 studies. Of which 73 have been organized through a three-way classification. One classification dimension is in terms of method and content. Five categories have been used: (1) a broad category labelled general management and supervision programmes which are taught by lectures and small group discussions and include material on labour relations, company policies, leadership, etc., (2) general human relations programmes employing conference methods and role playing, that deal with human relations problems of supervisors, (3) programmes that attempt to teach generalized problem solving and decision making skills (4) T-groups, sensitivity training, and laboratory education, and (5) specialized programmes which are devoted to very specific objectives such as increasing reading speed or reducing the halo error in appraisal system.

In addition, studies were classified according to whether internal or external criteria were used and whether the study employed 'some' or 'few' experimental controls. Internal criteria are outcome measures linked directly to the training content and assessed during or immediately after the learning or training experience, e.g., attitude measures, achievement tests, in-basket performance and opinion questionnaires. External criteria have been designed to assess behaviour changes in organizational role. The category "some" control meant the inclusion of a control or comparison group. "Few" controls have been defined as no control group but both have a pre-and post-measure for the trained group. In the three groups, the 73 studies have been grouped as shown in Table 1.

TABLE 1

Classification of Management Development Research Studies by Content Area, Types of Criteria, and Degree of Experimental Control

	External Criteria		*Internal Criteria*		
	Some Controls	*Few Controls*	*Some Controls*	*Few Controls*	*Total*
General Management Programmes	2	1	8	5	16

Contd.

General Human Relations Programmes	-	3	10	6	19
Problem Solving and Decision Making	-	1	3	-	4
F-groups and Laboratory Education	6	3	8	9	26
Speciality Programmes	5	-	3	-	8
Total	13	8	32	20	73

The majority of studies used internal criteria measures. In over 20 years of research only 21 studies used external criteria of behaviour changes. Of these 13 were what could be loosely described as controlled studies and 9 of the 13 controlled studies produced statistically significant difference on a major criterion variable.

Campbell et al (1970) drew a number of conclusions from these datas which are the following:

1. Approximately 80 per cent of the 35 studies in the first two content categories produced significant results but more than half of them used one particular measure i.e., an attitude measure of 'employee centredness' or 'consideration'. This was a narrow research view of Management Development.

   Schwartz, Stilwel and Scanlan (1968 a,b), in one of the best study of general management, used a time lag design to examine the effects of a university sponsored programme on management behaviour. The participants were split into two groups which were trained six months apart, thus the second group provided a control for the first group to be trained. The Leader Behaviour Description Questionnaire (LDBQ) was administered to the subordinates of each group before and after the programme. Managers in the first group were described as becoming less active, less definitive, less production centred, less oriented towards supervisors, and more oriented towards subordinates. In contrast, the second group was seen by subordinates as becoming more active, and using more structure. Apparently there was important interaction between the development programme and other parts of the organization such that the second group reacted differently than the first. This study used a feasible experimental design that provided considerable information.

Almost all other studies of general management and human relations training cited by Campbell et al (1970) provided considerably less information.

2. Perhaps more research was conducted on T-group and laboratory education than any other specific area. T-group studies accounted for nearly half of those utilizing external criteria. There is evidence that T-group produce behaviour changes in the work role for about 20-25 per cent of all participants.

The base of the external evidence for MD utility of laboratory education was found in perceived change studies. Five studies had been conducted by Boyd and Elliss (1962), Bunker (1965), Miles (1965), Underwood (1965), and Valiquet (1968). The primary dependent variable was an open-ended question which asked subordinates and/or associates of the experimental and control subjects, approximately a year after the laboratory experience, to describe specific changes they had observed in the subjects and/or behaviour in working with people during the previous year. All studies had at least one control group. Four of the five studies had chosen control subjects by asking the training participants to 'nominate' people similar to themselves. Experimental and control subjects, in turn, nominated several associates as observers.

Typical results were obtained in the study by Bunker (1965). Responses to the open-ended questions were content analyzed using 15 inductively derived categories. Eleven of the 15 sub-categories yielded statistically significant differences between the experimental and control group with the trained group showing greater change. The greatest differences (20%-25%) were in the areas related to increased openness, receptivity and tolerance of differences, increased skill in the interpersonal relationships and improved understanding of self and others. There were no differences for initiation of action, assertiveness and self-confidence.

While the results of these five studies seemed favourable, they must be qualified in view of the way control subjects and observers were selected. Also with the exception of Underwood (1965) the perceived changes were not evaluated in terms of their influence on job performance.

The T-group studies using internal criteria which were cited by Campbell et al (1970) produced mixed results. The evidence for laboratory-produced changes in self-awareness, inter-personal sensitivity, personality and performance on case problems or business games was negative. Some positive results were cited for the ability on T-groups to change certain kinds of attitudes but the data were not sufficient. In essence, the positive data with external criteria and negative data with internal criteria argued that it was not known what aspects of the training experience would produce the behaviour changes in the organization.

3. Only a few studies have been conducted on the attempts to teach problem solving and decision making skills and the results have been largely negative.

4. Studies comparing the relative effectiveness of two or more methods for the same goal or evaluating treatment interactions with individual differences were inadequate in number to offer any generalizations. Most of the emperical research dealt with just a few of the many possible methods.

5. In terms of methodological characteristics there was an almost exclusive reliance on statistical significance as a sign of changes to be interpreted. Hardly any study tried to link internal criterion changes with external criterion changes. Also, no study attempted to deal specifically with the effect of organizational structure or climate on training activities.

Using the laboratory methods O' Rourke and Castelli (1969) conducted relatively unstructured interview with the bosses of 72 supervisors six months after they had been in a T-group. The results seemed to indicate favourable changes in job performance but the study featured no control group, no before measure, and the bosses knew the reason for the interview. Zand, Steel and Zalking (1969) measured self perceived changes of manager's job behaviour by using a 42-items questionnaire. Pre and post-measures were employed but there was no control group. In terms of laboratory education objectives the post-measures went down but returned to the pre-training state when the sample was followed up a year after.

In one of the internal criterion studies, Rubin (1967) assessed changes in racial prejudice during a two-week T-group with a 15-items questionnaire that asked people to rank action alternatives in hypothetical situations. One of the two training groups were given a pre-measure two weeks before the T-group started. Thus the difference between the first and second pre-measures produce a decrease in the racial prejudice and the effect was greater for these and low on psychological anomic (measured by a 9-item Guttman scale). There was also a suggestion that the decrease in prejudice resulted from feelings of greater self acceptance. In another study Hall and Williams (1970) and 20 groups from each of three populations: student management and neuro-psychiatric patients, to study the effects of laboratory experience on group decision task the prediction of junior capitulation in the film 'Twelve Angry Men'. Half the groups were experimental and half the groups were controls and differences were examined on decision accuracy, degree to which the group used its individual resources, and the degree to which the group produced better predictions than any of its individuals. The laboratory appeared to facilitate this kind of decision making, but for some dependent variables, the effect was much greater for ad hoc groups than for established groups.

In four studies, Slocum (1968) demonstrated that college students reported on a pre vs post comparison that they were more sensitive and self-aware after a T-group; Finston (1969) used an interview to show that good, bad and so-so reactions to a T-group were distributed about equally in an R and D sample; Golembiewski and Blumberg (1967) showed rather weak attitudinal support for the positive effects of management confrontation experience; and Nadler and Fink (1970) demonstrated changes without a control group on questionnaire measures of broad democratic attitudes.

Laboratory education is a complex process. An increasing number of studies have attempted to explore this complexity. Varying the feedback parameter, Meyers and his associates (1969) asked participants at the end of each session in an eight session T-group to rate each other sociometrically and to predict how others would rate them. They were also given feedback as to how they were rated. The dependent variable was the accuracy of their predictions. One control group made the ratings but was not given feedback and another control group did nothing. The crucial determiner of accuracy was not feedback, but whether the participants rated other people. A study by French, Sherwood and Bradford (1966) tended to show that 'attending' to the variables to be rated produced almost as much change as feedback when the cue properties of the variables were removed there was a significant drop in rated change.

Culbert (1968) varied the amount of trainer self disclosure (i.e. high vs low) and noted its effects on the amount of individual 'self-awareness' exhibited in tape recordings of group sessions. There was an interaction between trainer disclosure and the stage training. To maximize self-awareness, as was rated by judges, the trainer should practice high self-disclosure at first and change to low self-disclosure later in the training. Cooper (1969) studied the effects of trainer attractiveness and the degree to which he exhibited behaviour congruent with T-group values. Participants who rated the trainer as attractive and congruent became more like him in both attitudes and behaviour (as judged from tapes).

Two studies explored the interaction of the T-group itself with other supporting experiences. Bunker and Knowles (1967) re-analyzed the original Bunker (1965) data and compared the results of two-week vs three-week laboratory programme where the only difference was in the time devoted to lectures, exercises and theory sessions. Time in the T-group remained constant. Results on the perceived change measure gave a significant advantage to the three-week programme. Friedlander (1968) used six questionnaire measures of work group functioning to study the effects of a laboratory programme. The content of the laboratory sessions varied considerably, but these differences were completely overshadowed by the amount of pre-training and post-training follow-up by the consultants. Friedlander also made some sharper comments about the reinforcement contingencies governing consultant behaviour and argued that they tended to encourage discrete, short term training experiences.

Lubin and Zuckerman (1969) used checklist measures of anxiety, depression and hostility to show that the level of emotional arousal in a T-group is not as great as in a perception isolation experiment.

Steele (1968) found no relationship between trainer rating of participant change and the Meyersbriggs Type Indicator. Harrison and Lubin (1965) demonstrated that 'task' oriented people were rated as learning more in a T-group than 'people' oriented participants.

The relationship of individual differences to T-group has been a neglected area of research. However, Buchanan (1969), Delbecq (1970) and Mangham and Cooper (1969) have interpreted the data on T-group researches.

General Management Programmes: Researches on general management have been conducted by Miller (1969), Kohan and Parker (1969), Thorley (1969) to name a few.

Human Relations Programme: Bartlett (1967) asked participants to play role parts antagonistic to their previously determined management style. This led to considerable discussion of the participants' organizational situation, and types of the discussions were fed back to top management. There was a subsequent reduction in organizational variables such as costs and absenteeism. Burke (1969) administered scales to measure Machievellianism and social attitudes before and after an undergraduate course in human relations. No changes were observed.

Problem Solving and Decision Making: There had been almost no attempts to study development of problem-solving and decision making skills during 1960s although a number of strategies existed for developing these skills. A study by Moore (1967) compared the business game vs case method in teaching problem-solving in production management. Very little difference was found between the two on an achievement examination.

The review shows that research again did not focus on management development from 1972 to 1980. However, trainability has been studied in the 1980s and success of a trainee has also been in focus of attention of researchers. One of the important criteria was knowledge about success of a trainee was given by Zink (1982) who demonstrated that a sampling of a trainee's ability level can be used as a valid predictor of subsequent success in training. In place of using miniature training, he showed that time spent early in a self-paced training course for Bell system service representatives could be used to determine training for students whose total training time was predicted to be excessively long. Specifically, time spent early in training was highly predicted to identify nearly 70 per cent of those who would exceed the maximum allowable time for course completion with a 'false alarm' rate of only 5 per cent. Trainability has been verified through a number of studies (e.g. Chides et al, 1981). One such prediction of success of trainees was developed by Tubiana and Ben-Shakhlar (1982) who developed and validated an objective group questionnaire for predicting success in Israeli Military training. The questionnaire focussed on personality and motivational factors (i.e., activeness, socialibility, responsibility, independence, promptness, motivation to serve in a combat unit) and, when combined with other predictors (e.g. level of intelligence, education, language, score), correlated 46 with training success.

A number of researches on environmental arrangements have been conducted so as to enable the trainer to control in order to facilitate such an amount of practice, task, sequencing, overlearning, feed-back and adapting to instruction to individual differences. Some of the studies belong to Instructional Psychology which deals with instructional procedures, techniques, and materials for transformation—from the initial state of the learner to the acquisition of competence as put forth by Glaser (1982). Hagman (1980) examined the effects of training task repetition of retention and transfer of maintenance skill. More than merely showing that trainees should be given the opportunity to practice what is being taught, this research suggested that there was an optimum number of task repetitions needed and this number would vary depending on training conditions.

Task sequencing has been studied for both cognitive and psychomotor skills. Gagne' and Briggs (1974) reported that the sequencing of cognitive skills has been based on a hierarchical approach to cognitive skills acquisition. The resulting theory is a structured learning hierarchy in which cognitive skills subordinate. Gagne' et al (1962) observed that the validity of this approach has been demonstrated using transfer of training techniques. Salvendy and Boydstun (1980) investigated the viability of a hierarchical model of psychomotor performance using two of

Fleishman's factors : control precision and rate control. Their results were inconclusive regarding the concept of a hierarchical structure for the acquisition of psychomotor skills. The establishment of hierarchical model would aid in the development of efficient acquisition procedures for those jobs involving psychomotor skills. Schendel and Hagman (1982) showed that over-training was superior to refresher training in combating forgetfulness, i.e., those soldiers trained to criterion who then received 100 per cent over training exhibited better retention than soldiers who were given the same amount of additional training midway through the retention intervals. The findings suggested that over-training may be a potent way of increasing effectiveness when sustaining psychomotor skills over a period fixed retention interval. This may be useful to training of technical psychomotor skills to engineers.

Mezoff (1982) provided a conceptual framework for a matching model approach to human relations training research. Based on an extensive review of literature on cognitive styles he hypothesized how persons of different cognitive styles would be differently responsive to structured (e.g., role plays, simulation games) and unstructured (e.g., T-group) human relations training. Training can use knowledge about participant's cognitive style to modify the design of focus on training. Large scale training programmes could group participants by cognitive styles and provide each group with a more individualized treatment.

Considering the importance of positive transfer for effective training in organizations, Baumgartel and his associates (Baumgartel et al 1978) worked on the nature of those factors which facilitate the adoption of new concepts and practices following MD programmes. Their findings showed that people in favourable organizational climates (e.g. high need achievement, high activity level) were more likely to adopt new practices. Climate has its greatest effect on persons with innovative dispositions; and this effect is more striking to persons at lower levels in organizational structure. Lefer and Newstrom (1980) and Michalak (1981) contended that positive transfer is maximised by a number of factors including continued interest and involvement by superiors, awareness of the obstacles to transfer, strategies for overcoming these obstacles, and reinforcement for maintenance of behaviour change.

Marx (1982) described a cognitive behavioural model that offered an integrated approach to the maintenance of behaviour. It was based on the relapse prevention (RP) model given by Marlett and Gordon (1980), which consisted of a set of self-control strategies to maintain abstinence from addictive behaviours such as smoking, alcoholism, and drugs. Although originally developed with addictive behaviours, the RP model appeared to have implications for the maintenance of managerial training. It involved making managers aware of the relapse process itself, asking them to pinpoint situations that are likely to sabotage their attempts to maintain new behaviour, and teaching them a variety of coping responses such as time management and delegative leadership style. An important empirical question that needed answering was whether a model designed to explain the long-term maintenance of addictive behaviours could be used for non-addictive behaviours learned in personnel training. The detailed description of the model is given in the following portion which deals with the theoretical models of management training.

Human Resource Development (HRD)

Odiorne (1985) reviewed the strategies for HRD in the 1970s and proposed changes in the strategies to be brought about during the 1980s in USA. Looking back over the last one decade, he reviewed that the personnel and HRD departments of organizations had focussed on the day to day operations that had lost sight of the future of the organizations and their human resources. Some discontent had prevailed during 1970s among the US top management on the performance in the personal areas. The major trends for 1980s in the USA had been spelt out by Odiorne (1985) for the near future were : (a) a move towards management by anticipation of future problems of HRD keeping in view cultural and social changes, (b) the motivational effects of physical plant design and layout would become an area of increasing interest, (c) more use of work team, (d) better strategies for managing managers and professionals, (e) treating employees as assets, (f) new systems for managing management information, (g) decentralization, (h) more socio-technical systems, (i) a giant step forward in training of employees and management training, (j) re-training, (k) adult education, and (l) customer education.

With the growth of behavioural technology new learning theories, new programmes, and methods of teaching have provided impetus to HRD. The technology of learning, according to Odiorne starts with a new set of definitions: "Training should change behaviour; behaviour is activity which can be seen or measured". Technological developments have resulted a perception of training as a major contributor to the HRD strategies of the organizations.

Salas (1985) investigated factors that facilitated or hindered the implementation of managerial technology in training, organizational development and performance measurement programmes in developing countries, through examination of decision making processes of managers at the macro-environment and organizational level. The study was conducted in Peru. Results identified the political, economic and socio-cultural factors that had a strong effect on managers when making decisions about implementing human resource development techniques. Specifically, quality of management and the blue collar employees, availability of local resources to support the technologies, top management commitment to HRD (which was one of the most important factors for success of HRD efforts), employee's commitment to organization, budget provisions for HRD, inflation, financial solvency of the company, and specific laws were found to be major determinants of decision making about implementation of a managerial technology in the study.

Margerison and Kakabadse (1985) conducted a research survey for training magazine using mailed questionnaire being sent to Chief Executives of 5000 U.S. companies. Of which, 717 chief executives responded (a 14 per cent response rate) from various industries. The questionnaire enlisted 21 key factors that contributed to the success of chief executives. Results showed that human relations, communication, planning, people management, and decision making were the areas where the MD training should emphasize. However, the results showed that the training was not adequate according to needs of the Chief Executives. The facts and figures gave the realistic picture of HRD efforts which needed closer attention and substantial efforts for making HRD useful to cater to the real needs of managers. Anderson (1986) offered a strategy for motivation in "Training" magazine. He came forward with the idea of self-esteem and suggested that self-esteem was what was needed to increase motivation in order to have increased productivity. Anderson argued that it was easy to assume that mature people would bring a healthy degree of self-respect and a well-developed sense of identity to the work-place. But what a boss said and thought about us still carried a great deal of weight. Anderson suggested five easy reminders for bolstering self-esteem. The suggestion to the managers was offered that if the self-esteem was given due importance, following the five tips, performance would be better and the subordinates would care for the productivity and for the organization.

Brinkerhoff (1986) emphasized expanding needs-analysis by redefining the function of needs analysis to realize organizational goals. In the past HRD was limited to training but the HRD has now expanded. Brinkerhoff (1986) redefined the needs-analysis and discussed at length the strengths of the models used to define the needs analysis and the relevance of needs analysis to meet the organizational development through achievement of organizational goals. The need analysis had gained more importance when heavy emphasis was given to HRD efforts. Needs analysis must establish the potential value of training efforts of the organization and relevance and real objectives for training must be found out. In the present day context needs analysis may provide us necessary insight in order to develop need-based training modules to cater adequately and usefully to the requirements of trainees.

Models and Theories

The origin of training may be traced basically to the learning theories and the 'learning principles' which are primarily the foundation for training in any area. Bass and Vaughan (1966), Blum and Neylor (1968) and Blum and Neylor (1984) have emphasized on learning principles. The learning principles have been given prominent place in major text books and they appear consistently in literature in the area of training; Hallestein (1969), and McCord

(1968) are the examples. The MD training programmes draw heavily their bases from the learning theory schools. Lippit and Bidwell (1971) gave prominance to the learning theories and emphasized the importance of learning theories which come to the rescue of the trainer to formulate and design suitable learning situation and conditions for appropriate learning of skills specific for the job tasks, which a learner has to perform on the job in his / her organization.

Learning theory is employed as a model for three areas of MD: (a) job redesign, (b) that Hawthrone studies, and (c) attitude formation and change towards labour unions. Analogies are drawn between the theoretical learning variables and variables in each of the three research areas. Balling (1982) proposed extensions of Neo-Hullian Learning Theory. Based on the analogies, Balling (1982) reduced a large number of predictions. He showed the learning theory to be capable of explaining a large portion of respective literature in these distinct research areas. He demonstrated the broader theoretical functions of research integration and research guidance by the use of an aesthetic theoretical tool employed in a highly functional theoretical technique. Gagne' (1962) highlighted the secondary importance of the principles of learning and observed that other considerations were more important. He made assumptions that total performance could be analyzed into a set of component tasks that were relatively distinct from each other. Further, proficiency on the task components mediated total performance. Based on these assumptions, the basic principles of training design consist of: (a) identifying the task components that make up the desired performance, (b) incorporate these component tasks of "mediators" in the training programme, and (c) arranging the learning of the components in the optimal sequence for transfer of total performance. This conceptualization implies that training practitioners and researchers should be concerned with task analysis, terminal behaviours, component task achievements, the fidelity of training task components, and sequencing. This conceptualization gives emphasis on the two basic questions: (a) what is to be learned, and (b) what the content of a training or development should be. Once answer to these basic questions is sought, additional questions of what techniques to use, mass vs distributed practice and how to reinforce learner responses will have to be considered. Gagne's statement could not stimulate training practitioners and researchers to the desired extent. Nevertheless, some work may be traced in the literature. In an attempt to answer the question what is to be learned, an earlier study by Glickman and Vallance (1958) had analyzed the descriptions of specific mistakes made by naval technicians on the job and used this information to alter training content. By using the critical incident method, the question was answered in terms of actual job behaviour and the specifications of training content followed directly. The systems approach developed later answered to these and other basic questions, but before that, a needs analysis is called for to have the knowledge whether there is really a need for training and by developing specific skills through a specific training programme.

Folley (1969) determined the desired behaviours of retail sales personnel by collecting critical incidents from customers. More than 2000 incidents were collected, categorized and made the basis for training in customer service. Similar attempts were made by Buehler (1969) who developed a series of selected critical job behaviour incidents that defined the "desirability for retention" of clerical personnel. In fact it was an analysis of total performance into its components. Harmon (1968) discussed a more molar approach for specifying behaviours to be learned. He presented an analysis of performance objectives for job Corps curriculum development. Fourteen objectives were grouped under three major headings: verbal performance, physical performance, and attitudinal performance. Each of these objectives was explained by descriptions of the desired behaviour, the conditions under which the desired behaviour should occur and the success criteria by which the trainee's behaviour is to be judged.

The content of the management development literature illustrates the difficulties generated by deviation from behavioural specifications of what is to be learned. Hersey and Kellner (1968) reviewed many underlined theories, such as the theory of need achievement implies that training should create a high achievement need. Theory X vs Theory Y suggests manager should be taught the versatile use of Theory Y. The Herzberg's two factors theory proposes that supervisors should learn to use intrinsic factors to motivate subordinates. Likert's system-Four suggests that participative and consultative approach to management is the best. The original Ohio State variables of consideration and initiating structure appear most forcefully in the Management Grid Approach. They propound that managers should be taught a style that maximizes both a concern for production and concern for people. Reddin (1967, 1968, 1969) argued that style theories were not useful as they implied an either/or approach using either the ideal or non-ideal style and they structured the world in terms of a few types instead of several gradations on a continuum. He also emphasized that the grid must be made three dimensional and agreed that each combination of employees and production - centredness could vary in an "effectiveness" dimension, i.e., there may be situations in which even a 1,9,9,1 or 5,5 may be effective. This implies that a manager's use of various styles must take account of situational and individual differences. Hersey and Blanchard (1969) have also argued that proper mix of production-centredness and employee considerations depend in a large degree on the developmental stage in the life-cycle of the work group. Common (1969) also made the Grid three dimensional by postulating a commitment dimension which implied that training should take account of individual differences in the probability of using various systems.

In a study on a organizational climate as determining factor in managerial training carried out by Schoombee (1980), one of the results was that in the public sector no sign of a dominant managerial style and that the influence of the organizational climate on the organization, and on the individual managers was such that they lost their particular managerial style. These findings may not be generalized globally but, as reported in the African conditions, they may also be applicable to Indian conditions since the bureaucratic set up and job security in addition to organizational factors also play an important role in the public sector organizations in India.

The definitions of the variables, however, do not provide a clear specification of what the desired behaviour are or what the training content should be to ensure acquisition of the component tasks. Determining of training content, thus, is an inferential step. The content of the training programme could be decided by programmed instruction and computer assisted instruction. However, Frank and Smith (1969) observed that task analysis and behavioural specifications training objectives seemed to be much more prevalent.

Attitude Theory: The content of learning or training may be considered as a particular set of attitudes, beliefs, or options. There is emphasis on attitudes in training activities such as supervisory attitudes towards employees or Supervisors attitudes towards minority group. Shaw and Wright (1967) has compared all the major definitions of attitudes and discussed the theoretical and psychometrical issues in measurement. They systematically reviewed attitude scales. A book edited by Fishbein (1967) gives comprehensive readings on attitude theory and measurement of attitudes. Rokeach (1968) reviewed the literature on attitude change. He distinguished attitudes from other concepts and presented his own comprehensive theory of attitudes. Keisler, Collins and Miller (1969) discussed five major types of attitude change theories.

Motivation Theory : Learning and motivation go hand in hand. Parmeswaran (1983) has discussed that learning and motivation are although independent psychological processes, yet they are inter-related and are influenced by each other. Perception is also one such cognitive process. Effective learning depends on adequate motivation and many motives are the results of learning. In the context of training all these processes play an important role. Studies of Locke' and his associates offered a number of important points. Locke' (1967) and Locke' et al (1968) suggested that the effects of reinforcement on learning may be mediated by a process of goal-setting. Unless the learner changes his goals in the training situation, reinforcement such as knowledge of results, money, and recognition may have no effect. They also suggested that adopting a specific goal as opposed to 'do the best' goals results in greater effort and perhaps better response acquisition. Locke' (1966) reanalyzed the Fryer's data dealing with learning Morse Code and demonstrated that those who said that they set high goals acquired correct responses faster than those who set low goals or no goals at all. Konwin (1967) showed the same results with field operatives in a stockings factory. The training programme was geared to teaching girls to pace themselves with goal setting. Production went up and turnover went down. Campbell (1970) argued that effects of goal setting may be due to its task definition component, i.e., performance is enhanced because in the process of setting a goal the individual learns what he is supposed to do, whereas the task previously may have been unclear. Thus, as a training device performance appraisal means of mutual goal setting may be effective because it allows the subordinate to bring order to a previously ambiguous situation. This may be explanation for the results of a study of T-group training by Kolb, Winter and Berlew (1968) which showed that when subjects who were graduate students set personal training goals, there were more self and trainer perceived changes. The stronger the commitment to the goal, the more changes were perceived. Thus, the datas are suggestive of giving special consideration to how goal setting could be used in training and management development programmes.

Campbell, Dunnette, Lawler and Welk (1970) postulated and cited evidence for the motivational influence of the individual's degree of belief or expectancy that could accomplish a particular goal or master a particular task. Thus, an individual's expectations of how well he will be able to handle the training content may have a bearing on his motivation in the training situation. The expectancy-valence model is the strongest in the theories of work motivation to explain the motivation in training situation and has considerable potential utility for training and development. Porter and Lawler (1968), and Locke' (1969) have elaborated the use of VIE model.

Behaviour Modification : Bandura (1969) has given a definitive treatment of behaviour modification principles and the technique. Behaviour modification model has exclusively been applied to neurotic, psychotic, or delinquent behaviours. However, the concept and techniques are general and the model could have served as a powerful training model in organizations. Ullman and Krasner (1965) have given a brief and less definitive treatment of behaviour modification model. Mehrabian (1970) gave a popularized version of the model.

Behaviour modification is based partially on the Skinnerian and Pavlovian principles of conditioning. It goes beyond these principles and has utilized many basic findings of learning theories. It seeks to change individual responses by changing the individual's environment and by altering reinforcement contingencies on stimulus pairings. It is the behaviour which is important and not the underlying causes or internal mediators. The model proposes the following processes:

(a) The training objectives must be carefully specified in terms of specified desired behaviours.

(b) The existing reinforcement contingencies must be carefully described for the purposes of alteration.

(c) New contingencies or pairings must be selected that will directly support the desired behaviour. The new reinforcers must be powerful enough to alter behaviour and to maintain it once it has been changed.

(d) Change agents must be selected to administer the reinforcement.

(e) If the desired behaviour is seldom elicited or it is too complex to be reinforced contiguously, sub-goals must be reinforced contiguously and sub-goals must be shaped.

(f) After the behaviour has been altered, provisions must be made for making it self regulating.

Baundura (1969) described six methods of instituting new contingencies: (a) modelling and vicarious processes, (b) positive reinforcement, (c) negative reinforcement, (d) extinction, (e) positive counter conditioning, and (f) aversive counter conditioning. Bandura (1969) treated each of the six at length, examples were given, and the possible uses and limitations of each was discussed. For organizational settings a combination of modelling and positive reinforcement would seem to be useful for training situations. The learner is shown a model who acts in a desired fashion and is reinforced. The learner is then reinforced for eliciting behaviour similar to that of the model. Thus many behaviours which previously were not the learner's behaviour can be generated and reinforced. Bandura (1969) discussed at length moral and ethical issues related to behaviour modification. In the social setting it is possible and also desirable that the change agent and learner agree on the reinforcement contingencies to be used and Bandura gave evidence to show that an individual's awareness of the contingencies involved had an enhancing rather than distracting effect. He suggested a number of organizational applications. The main problem lies in selecting relevant reinforcers and being able to apply them directly and skillfully to elicit the desired behaviour, e.g., instead of a human relations training for supervisors in order to convince them of the desirability of acting in certain ways with their subordinates, we may provide them with the correct behaviour with highly valued rewards. It would require a radical reorientation in organizational life and substantial applications of behaviour modification principles are not possible. However, data reviewed by Bandura suggests that the incredible power of the technique and some try-out has been done. Perhaps the employment problems of "hardcore" workers may be solved by application of this technique.

It is noteworthy to mention here that Nord (1969) argued that the operant conditioning model has great structural similarity to the motivation theories of McGregor, Maslow and Herzberg.

Individual Differences: Gagne's (1967) showed the importance of individual differences in learning. The individual differences play an important role in learning process. Cronbach (1967) conceptualized the problem of how instruction could be adapted to individual differences. He discussed about adaptation with fixed goals and fixed methods adaptation by matching the instructional methods to the individual, and adaptation by selecting homogenous groups. He suggested that two individual variables of prime importance were general mental ability and the need achievement fear of failure configuration. Evidence was cited by him to support his view. Glaser (1967) made a distinction between the traditional kinds of individual difference measures, and "initial states" and argued that initial states were potentially more interactive than traditional kind of individual difference measures. Thus variables like prior achievement, training expectations, and initial skill level are more potent than aptitude, interest, or personality measures. Lundberg (1966) outlined some potentially important initial state variables for Management Development (MD).

Jensen (1967) specifically rejected more than 40 individual difference measures developed from factor analyses and suggested a new taxonomy for explaining the error variance in training results. Perhaps the most important distinction made by Jensen (1967) was between intrinsic variables or individual differences in the learning process themselves, and extrinsic variables which had an effect on learning outcomes but they had no resemblance to the learning process itself. Fleishman (1967) summarized sizable amount of data he produced on individual differences in psychomotor learning and made a distinction between abilities as relatively enduring traits and skills as levels of proficiency of specific tasks. His objective was to explain task performance skills through the underlying abilities. He developed a taxonomy of psychomotor and motor abilities. A number of studies using different methodologies were used to support that the ability requirements for a task performance change considerably over the training period since, as learning progresses, the nature of the task changes. Also, as the number of trial increases, an increasingly larger proportion of total variance is explained by factors specific to the task itself. Fleishman (1967) suggested that the ability variables which correlates highly with task performance at various training stages indicate the instructional cues, or content emphasized at each stage. Anderson (1967) disagreed with the suggestion and argued that ability correlations were not as useful as a rigorous task analysis itself for specifying training content. Hulin and Alvarez (1970) followed a more radical approach and argued that individual's ability level indeed might not be constant and might be explained by changes in ability factors as well as task factors.

Factors analysis of ability tests included in the same matrix with performance scores over trials had also been used to demonstrate the increasing importance over trials and one which decreases. However, the factor loadings were somewhat different across samples and conformed to expectations based on the instructional sets. The impact of these results is weakened by Humphrey's earlier paper (1960) who had suggested that including trial X trial data in a correlation matrix might anti-factually yield an increasing task specific factor and a decreasing task specific factor.

General System Theory: The systems approach was widely used, e.g., Miller (1969) applied systems concept to training. Berrien (1968) explained the General Systems Theory (GST). According to Berrien (1968) GST was that which should have considerable heuristic value. Berrien (1968) distinguished between two types of systems inputs: maintenance vs signal, two types of systems outputs: usable vs waste, and among three concepts, viz., system growth, adaptation, and learning. GST led to certain deductions about the relationship of sub-systems, e.g., the training function to the supra-system or the organization. A sub-system cannot survive if all its outputs must be directly usable by the supra-system. A number of useful strategies for the training practitioner may emerge from the systems approach.

Organizational Development

Organizational Development (OD) is a comparatively new approach which takes into account a broader range of system considerations towards training and development. OD has taken into account the Management Grid approach also which was expanded and codified by Blake and Mouton (1968, 1970). It consists of six phases from the Grid Seminar to a formal critique phase. A second type of OD approach is labelled "action research". A paper by Beer (1969) gives a description of what is meant by this term with examples. The process is that the "change agent" must first search the organization for the most fertile ground in which to plant his initial developmental effort. Concomitantly he must collect data that tell him if he is on the right track, guide future efforts, and demonstrate the worth of the method to the rest of the organization. If the data are positive, the change effort can be expanded and more data be collected. The basic approach is that the content of the change effort is not important but the ever-expanding cycle of action-data process. The process was described by Zaner (1968). A third major thrust of OD is system-four management as described by Likert (1967). It is an organization-wide attempt to install participative and consultative management by means of conference techniques and the feed-back of diagnostic questionnaire results. Laboratory education has been modified increasingly to include groups sampled from a vertical or diagonal slice of the organization described by Benedict et al (1967). Thus the inter-personal difficulties, communication problems, and inter-level conflict that hinder organizational functioning, can be faced directly.

Interventional Theory : Clark (1975) described four models of intervention strategies in terms of the expectations of practioner and client, and the different conditions were suggested in which each model might be most appropriate : (a) The collaborative/ diagnostic model which has a number of variations—mutual determination of goals and joint effort in voluntary relationship, maximum participation by those affected by change or joint discussion of policy, joint evaluation of alternatives, and utilization of action research by the client for diagnosis and other activities, (b) the unilateral expert model seems inappropriate for in-depth interventions designed to bring about changes in attitudes, (c) the delegated or do-it-yourself model well-known in the area of work simplification, is required for some aspects of the use of Blake and Mouton's managerial grid and (d) the subordinate technician model in which the client specifies the service required, the practitioner then obtains and reports the information to the client, who then decides on the next step(s).

Models of Management Development : Doraiswami (1983) described and analyzed a number of Management Development (MD) models, viz., the Administration Model, the Synthesizing Model, the Problem-Solving Model, the Marketing Model, and the Integrated Model. The Integrated Model takes into consideration all the aspects of Management Development (MD) and includes psychological processes such as perception, motivation and increase in knowledge and skill (which may be brought about through training). Each model has already been discussed in the preceding chapter (MD training approaches).

Relapse Prevention (RP) Model : Marx (1986) developed a Relapse Prevention (RP) Model based on the phenomenon that the skills carefully shaped during MD training do not survive the transition to the work-place. As high as 90 per cent relapse rate has been reported. Feed-back from trainees indicated that the complex behaviours frequently taught in management development seminars actually comprise numerous support skills. The support skills facilitate behaviour change. Support skills differ among individuals. When deficit occurs in even one key support skill it is less likely that the new behaviour will last much beyond the training period. The RP Model proposed by Marx (1986) is useful as a diagnostic tool for identifying necessary support skills and as a training intervention which can increase long term skill retention. The managers, who are often enthusiastic and highly motivated during training, encounter a completely different and unsupportive environment upon returning to work. A key assumption of the model is that learning will be retained more effectively if the uncertainty of the post-training environment is reduced. This is accomplished in several ways. During the training the managers are trained in several strategies to help reduce the unpredictability of skill retention. These strategies are categorised into four steps of behavioural self-management: (a) Stimulus situation, (b) Thoughts and feelings of the individual (organism), (c) Behaviour, and (d) Consequences of the behaviour. The systematic training of RP is a learning by doing type, which enables the trainees to identify the problem areas, identify support skills that will prevent relapse to the old ways, and remedies are also suggested that are tried by the trainees. Thus, every step is an exercise and the trainee learns to practice the strategies on return to work after completion of training.

Multi-Faced System for Development : Mahler and Wrightnour (1973) proposed a multifacet model for development. The model is self-explanatory. The multifacet model provides opportunity to select from the college level suitable students to be trained by the organization and later after a satisfactory performance, may be absorbed in the organization's management to have the best suited personnel in management of the organization.

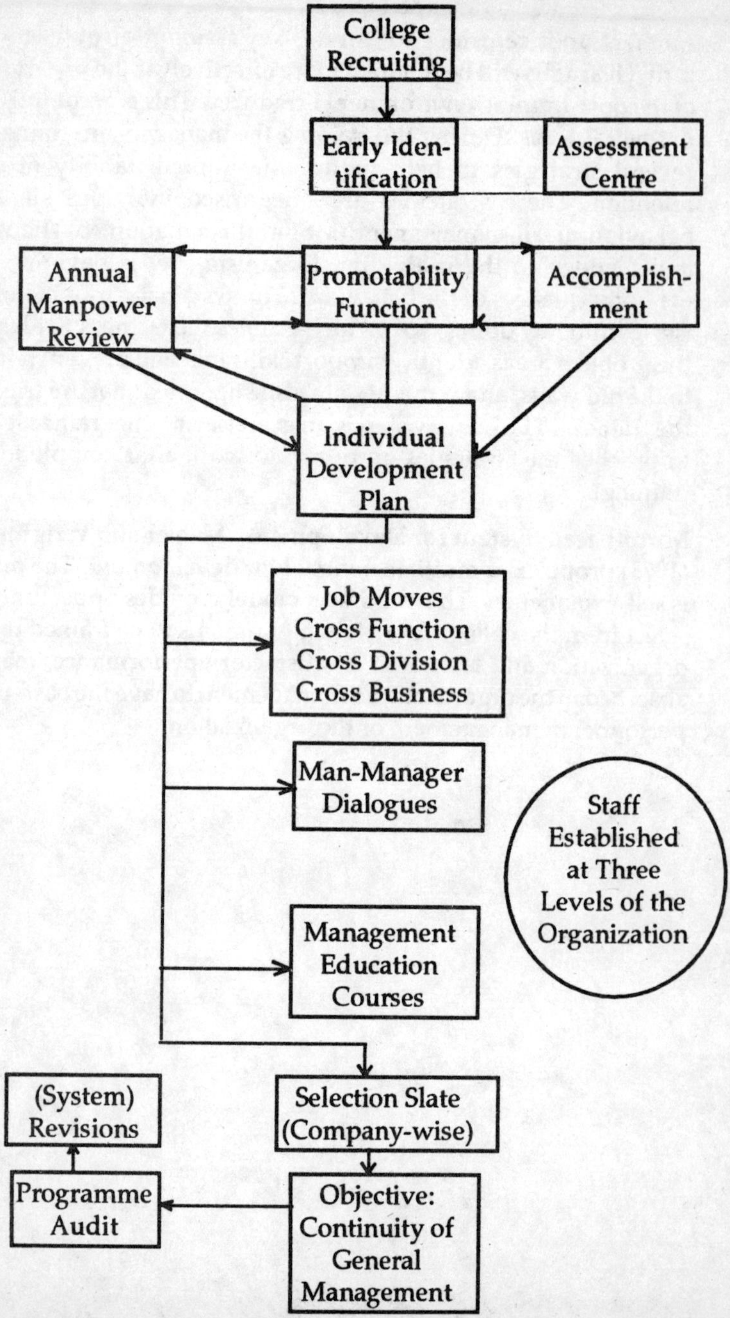

A multifaceted system for development. {In selecting and Developing only the Best Employees: Judson Smith, Training, Vol. 15, No. 9, 1978 (September), (pp. 21-24), (page 22)}.

Job Design and Job Aids

An additional outcome of a job study is the recommendations that are often made about restructuring the job to make them easier to learn, developing efficiency to perform, and making the jobs more interesting and enjoyable. Poock (1969) suggested that even simple changes in the design of equipments, such as colour coding and rearrangement of controls can make a task easier to learn and perform. Similar to this is the approach to design job aids that simplify a job by providing ready references and guides for the job procedures. Job aids are particularly useful in infrequently performed complex procedures or where there is little need for rapid or emergency performance. The job aids simplify the tasks of training since an employee can be trained to use the job aid in contrast to perform a complex procedural task by memory.

Job Design : Taylor (1911) first propounded the systematic approach to design jobs to increase worker effectiveness, referred to as scientific management, which attempted to identify the "one best way" of doing a job. Scientific management attempted work simplification and specialization. The approach scientifically offered simplification of job design and need for job enlargement was felt since work was over-simplified. Scientifically managed jobs were highly structured. The procedure of performing the job was explained to the worker as also the limit desired in performance of that job task. In order to motivate employees scientific management relied on financial incentives. According to Taylor (1911) : "whenever the workman succeeds in doing his task right, and within the time-limit specified he receives an addition of from 30 per cent to 100 per cent to his ordinary wages".

Job Enlargement : Job enlargement primarily focussed on increasing the number of activities of workers in which they were engaged. Job enlargement theorists often prescribed increasing discretion over work methods. Most of the applications of job enlargement focussed directly on providing a wider range of activities. In job enlargement programmes, instead of performing one simplified task, the tasks were usually of similar difficulty to one another, which resulted in horizontal loading of the job. Job enlargement was popular from late 1940s to early 1960s. Griffin (1982) reported that researches used to document the effectiveness of these programmes were often inadequately designed but cumulative evidence suggests that satisfaction and quality of performance increased. On the other hand, both training costs and job ability requirements increased. Quantity of performance appears to have been relatively unaffected.

Job Enrichment : Job enrichment provided probably the greatest impetus for job design and was evolved in the 1960s. Job enrichment approach focussed on providing opportunities for employee growth through vertical job loading which introduced a greater depth of responsibility. Herzberg (1959) had proposed Motivation-Hygiene Theory popularly known as Two-Factor of Motivation. Herzberg's work was the driving force behind the job enrichment. Job enrichment became popular and like job enlargement most of the researches on the effectiveness of job enrichment had research design problems. The effectiveness and limitations of the approach, therefore, proved difficult to be reported accurately. Aldag and Brief (1979) argued that job enrichment approach fails to provide an adequate framework for identifying the strength and weakness of a job so that changes can be made to improve it. Case Studies (Herzberg, F., 1977: Orthodox Job Enrichment. Defense Management Journal, 13, 21-27; Herzberg, F. and Rafalco, F.A. 1975: Efficiency in the military : cutting costs with orthodox job enrichment. Personnel, 52, 38-48) of job enrichment applications have, however, shown that the approach has potential and the job enrichment model provided thrust for more recent job design approaches.

Job Characteristics : Job characteristics study was carried out by Turner and Lawrence (1965). Six attributes related to worker attributes which showed relationship to worker attitudes and to a lesser extent related to worker attendance were : (a) variety, (b) autonomy, (c) required interaction, (d) optional interaction, (e) knowledge and skill required and (f) responsibility. These six characteristics were fairly consistent with combined set of job factors which had been used by job enlargement and job enrichment perspectives. Worker values were important factor that had role in job enrichment for the job design. Hackman and Lawler (1971) identified four core job characteristics : variety, autonomy, task identity and feed-back and two less critical characteristics were: dealing with others, and friendship opportunities. They developed a measure of higher-order outcomes such as personal growth and accomplishment in an attempt to identify the reasons for some workers to respond more positively to job characteristics than the others. The results indicated that greater amounts of job characteristics were associated with more positive worker reactions. It was also found that workers with strong higher-order need strength respond mostly to job characteristics (Dunham, 1984) Hackman and Oldham (1975) developed the Job Diagnostic Survey, a measure of job characteristics and the Growth Need Strength scale, which was meant for measurement of individual characteristics. Growth Need Strength is the degree to which a person desires complex, challenging work. The core job characteristics combine to influence psychological states like experienced meaningfulness of the work, experienced responsibility for outcomes of the work, and knowledge of the actual results of work activities.

Quality of Work Life (QWL): The QWL has been defined in the organizational and work context as the degree to which members of a work organization are able to satisfy important personal needs through their experiences in the organization. The definition implies that the QWL can be assured by measures of need importance and need satisfaction and it suggests that the two types of factors that largely determine QWL are : (a) those that influence the importance of a particular need to an individual, and (b) those that satisfy or frustrate a need. The QWL of an individual is determined not only by personal or situational characteristics alone but by the interaction between these two sets of factors by the close interaction of individual with the organization. The definition also implies that the basic strategy for improving QWL is first to identify and then try to satisfy people's most important needs presumably through their experience in their work environment.

The concept of QWL is, thus, based on the assumption that individual's own experience of satisfaction or dissatisfaction defines the QWL. The characteristics of work situation induce corresponding attitudes of satisfaction or dissatisfaction. The association between working conditions and satisfaction is not always constant; it is moderated by attitudes of the individual that bear upon his abilities, values and expectations. Thus attitudes can be probably the potent factors in modifying behaviour and individual differences in relation to job qualities. Measures of QWL must, therefore, consider the role of satisfaction and satisfaction should be treated as a cause and not merely a consequence of QWL. The QWL refers to the interaction between individual employees and their organisation. The needs of employees for material rewards and chances to learn and grow must somehow be meshed with the needs of the organization for attaining goal of productivity, creativity, reliability, loyalty, and high performance. Job enrichment may be the part of diverse changes that might be thought to be brought in order to achieve the goal of increasing QWL. According to Davis and Cherns (1975) progress has been made in providing work environments protecting the worker's physical well being; however, there is little agreement on what kind of working conditions and organizational practices are important to provide a psychologically good work life, i.e., to maintain their mental health and sense of well being. Poor individual/organization environment fits produce dissatisfaction and a psychologically poor work environment. Behavioural outcomes produced by psychologically harmful job are high rate of turnover, absenteeism, mental illness, tension-related physical illness, and alcoholism. Job satisfaction, alienation and motivation are important to obtain information on QWL in organisation.

The QWL is directly related to the needs of individuals. There is, therefore, necessity to apply needs analysis to gain knowledge about individual's and organizational needs so that both may be meshed together for growth and development of employee as well as organization. Brinkerhoff (1986) emphasized on expanding needs analysis by redefining the function of needs analysis to realize organizational goals. According to Brinkerhoff when the HRD was only training, needs analysis was an easier task. But HRD has expanded and while some HRD will represent the classic training definition since HRD is being increasingly viewed as a "perk" of training process. Needs analysis is applied only when the training fits the available definition. Training needs analysis should be conducted during the skill development efforts during the training. Training needs analysis poses a basic contradiction, i.e., a training needs analysis presumes that there is already a need for training. It must ask whether training, or something else might be useful for a need or problem or whether training plus something else is required. Mager and Pipe (1970) and Rumler (1976) have mentioned that in order to avoid providing training to meet non-training problems, needs analysis has been constructed as a "problem solving" effort. Brinkerhoff further argued that the current and potential worth of HRD was beyond finding in an organization for something which had gone wrong. In addition to remediating performance, weaknesses and deficits the HRD could enhance the strengths, seek out and serve opportunities for greater performance, anticipate and avoid future problems, and create new strengths. Available definitions and concepts of needs analysis were witnessed to be inadequate for such goals.

It is necessary to recognize the value component of need for expanded understanding of need analysis. When it is said that something is needed means that it is necessary or useful in serving some valued purpose. For example, money by itself meets no need but has utility in gaining things that are valued. Similarly, training by itself provides no outcome that has intrinsic value: the value of training outcomes may be established only relative to the degree that they serve or are useful for achieving something that the organization values. Thus, need analysis must establish the potential value of training effort to the organization and needs analysis must answer these basic questions: (a) what good, if any, can training do? and (b) How valuable, relative to other possible "goals", is the "good" that training do? Need analysis closely relates to evaluation. Stufflebeam (1977) reviewed many examples of need analysis in various fields and identified four useful definitions of need. Each definition fitted different training situations, leads to different training value bases, and implies the use of different need analysis methods, viz., discrepancy, democratic, diagonostic, and analytic needs. Discrepancy is defined as a difference between an ideal normative or expected level of performance and actual level of performance. By comparison needs may be identified. The identification of discrepancy needs requires a quantifiable expected level and a measure for actual performance. A democratic need is the preference by the majority. People may not be aware of the fact or want that someone else believes about their needs. Participation in the needs definition process generates commitment and acceptance and can enhance performance in later training. Diagnostic needs are defined through research and causal analysis. HRD should concern itself with what is right in an organization as well as what is wrong. Concentrating HRD resources on deficits will allow strengths to deteriorate. Analytic needs are discovered by intuition, insight, expert consideration and enlightenment. Analytic needs lead to new levels of performance. Analytic need may not be valid and may be hard to justify and support because of its dependence on individual or small group. The HRD efforts must make note of all four types of needs. Different organization contexts and situations will call for differing needs approaches and any given situation will benefit from a multiple needs analysis perspective. From an organizational perspective the HRD function should operate and be guided by policy that encourages use of all need definitions. The Quality of Work Life (QWL) can be improved by using needs analysis in an organization.

Use of system to describe and develop human resources has been used during the past decade. Systems provide a logical and thorough approach. In human resource development systems method has been utilized in the design of instructional systems so as to meet the needs of groups. Use of systems approach would facilitate to find out specific objectives of a training programme.

Clark (1975) discussed four models of intervention strategies in terms of the expectations of practitioner and client and suggested different conditions in which each model may be most appropriate. These models are: collaborative, diagnostic, delegated and subordinate technician models.

It is evident from the panorama of studies cited above that most of the studies have been conducted on shop floor workers and on those in junior supervisory level. However, attention is also given to models of intervention strategies and management process, e.g. Doraiswami (1983) discussed different models of management process: (a) administration model, (b) synthesizing model, (c) problem solving model, (d) marketing model and (e) integrated model. Parmeswaran (1982) emphasized on the importance of psychological approaches to human behavior which have much to contribute in MD training and solutions to many a ticklish problems, lies under these psychological approaches. Therefore, we cannot afford to neglect the psychological approaches.

Indian Studies

In India academicians from diverse disciplines, top management and management trainers have recognized the importance of management development training in the past few decades, especially a growing concern was witnessed in the early eighties. Efforts have been made to develop approaches to management which may specifically be suited to Indian context and the Indian industrial organizations. In the early eighties the trend was to regard MD crucially important. There was thrust of conceptualizations centering around the optimization of human resources development through MD functions. Of these, the most important function has been MD training. In the late eighties the concept of HRD has gained sufficient attention and concern, and the late eighties has experienced a kind of flood of literature in the field of HRD. The academicians and scholars from diverse academic disciplines have paid attention to analyze variety of HRD problems at different levels. Articles, bocks and proceedings of seminars on different aspects of HRD could provide an overall view and included valuable contributions from social scientists, but unfortunately the more comprehensive view of HRD has not served the desired objectives in terms of composite content and perspective. The academic exercises could not specifically focus to offer solutions to the experienced problems, especially in the public sector organizations. High costs, low productivity, heavy losses are constantly posing threat to the very idea of mixed economy as a result of which public sector was conceptualised and enterprises were set up by the government to accelerate the process of economic development through industrialization in the country. Sick public sector units especially need to be paid greater attention and efforts should focus to alleviate sick public sector organizations from the present unfortunate condition of being on the verge of closure.

Review of literature of the seventies shows that in public sector organizations the top management and the government failed to recognize the importance of Management Development training. The results in present day context are, therefore, discouraging. It is quite evident from the condition of sick public sector units today. The answer to deal with these problems lies in different aspects of conceptual framework which provides an insight into underlying causes which require emergent and more focussed attention. Doraiswami (1983), Amarchand (1983), Pareek (1983), Agarwal (1983), Fernandes (1983), De (1983), Raman (1983), and Venkataratnam (1983) are to name a few who have dealt with different aspects of conceptual framework for MD training in public sector organizations and have offered probable solutions to existing problems.

The Indian studies may be broadly classified into the eight areas, namely conceptual framework, functional areas, performance criteria, methodological issues, approaches and policies, need for MD training, effectiveness of training, and training evaluation. Table 2 shows the broad areas of studies:

TABLE 2

Broad Areas of Indian Studies

Area	*Number of Studies*
Conceptual framework	1
Functional areas	5
Performance criteria	1
Methodological issues	4
Approaches and policies	10
Need for MD training	6
Effectiveness of training	1
Training evaluation	5
Total	33

Table 2 shows that maximum studies related to the area of approaches and policies. The second priority area which came into focus of attention was need for MD training. Studies on training effectiveness and training evaluation have critically reported that the MD training was not satisfactory and serious efforts were required (e.g., Ganguly, 1983). The following few paragraphs give an account of studies in different areas.

Doraiswami (1983) illustrated the management process in terms of five different models of management in modified form. In each model certain inputs were added as a modification. The integrated model of management involved multiple capabilities such as analysis, forecasting, motivation, perception, innovation, problem-solving, satisfying and surviving. Discussing the various requirements for management development, Doraiswami (1983) suggested the strategy for MD through training and education. He discussed about essential factors which were conducive to MD and emphasised on their institutionalization. Doraiswami concluded that MD would be judged mainly by its ability to revive and reinforce commitment to achievement and excellence.

Amarchand (1983) emphasized on need for MD training in public enterprises. He enlisted methods of MD training and the course contents of training modules.

Pareek (1983) stressed on the social responsibility of business organizations and an organization was viewed by Pareek (1983) as an agent for bringing about changes through its training and development activities which should not necessarily be confined within the organization. The organization should interact with educational and non-educational institutions, plan for planned interventions and can sponsor or even run institutions of various kinds. Pareek also proposed a spiral model of training process having multiple type of involvement of the organization. In addition to process interventions he emphasized on structural interventions leading to organizational development. Behaviour change may be brought about through learning situations offering change for ample practice to learn.

Parmeswaran (1983) emphasized on the psychological approaches to behaviour and considering the importance of psychological factors and individual differences stressed on the application of psychological approaches to management development training. The basic objective of MD training, as defined by Parmeswaran, is to develop effective managers and well adjusted human beings.

Ragahvaiah (1983) analyzed the present situation of training of managers in public enterprises and concluded that effective and meaningful training for public sector managers would be possible only when the training function is recognized by policy makers and senior management as a necessary component of MD process. Fernandes (1983) discussed some critical issues arising from the question of building up trained cadres of public enterprises managers and devising of training policies, strategies, and methodologies purposefully oriented towards this objective.

Venkataratnam (1983) highlighted the critical importance of developing executive skills in public sector organization managers to make them self-reliant in managerial resources. He discussed several issues and concluded that the present system of maintenance of data on managerial talent, scanning, retrieving and presentation of information needed further refinement of manpower planning.

Fernandes (1983) related training to manpower planning, recruitment, career planning, wage policy, incentives, industrial relations, and motivation. He emphasized linkages of training in MD to education system.

De (1983) quoted a cross-cultural study by Smith and Thomas (1967) with a group of 164 senior and middle level Indian managers. De (1983) quoted other studies also by several researchers and concluded that effective team work was rather weak among Indian managers.

Raman (1983) proposed MD programmes for different levels of management (e.g., junior management, middle management and senior management levels). He expressed his point of view that a successful MD programme had to be built around the existing managerial environment and an understanding of managerial effectiveness both at micro and macro levels. He suggested that such an understanding could be provided by first exposing the managers en masse in an organization to the models described by him. The main result, according to Raman, expected from an understanding and implementation of the approach was the "development" of "individual" managers who perceived not only their individual role but also the organizations' objectives through an integrated and unified approach. This would result in manager's identifying the actions to be taken individually and through the involvement of appropriate private staff functions in the organization.

Agarwal (1983) discussed MD training problems in the public sector and emphasized on making management training more effective and objective and goals should be thought out carefully as large amount of public fund was invested in the public sector. An investment in training must pay-off sizeably in increased productivity, efficiency, morale and profits. The importance of training should be realized by top management since this alone could be a line of successful personnel for the future of the organization and the nation.

Chowdhary (1983) considered determination of training needs and methods in terms of development goals and welfare objectives of public enterprises. Determination of training needs and methods should be reviewed as a continuous process. The knowledge skills and attitude/values had been considered by Chowdhary (1983) as some among the requirements which were critically needed by managers for the effective management of public enterprises. The requirement suggested by Chowdhary in the present context was on an overall strategy, and the organisational goals meant to administer that strategy in Bangladesh, as cited by the researcher of this study, to serve as an example, for all developing countries.

Functional areas of MD training, as described by practitioners, are: training of internal auditors, training of corporate planning, training in materials management, management in public sector banks, training and development of women executives.

Khandelwal (1983) defined the internal audit and its role in public enterprises. He also discussed the required skills of an internal auditor. The trained internal auditor would meet the requirements under the changed environment of business would be effective and successful through the indispensable utility of skilled services to management leading to the improvement in the efficiency of management. In future the internal auditor would be an essential tool of "productivity movement" in the country. Khandelwal (1983) also suggested courses for training of internal auditors.

Chakraborty (1983) adopted the perspective that corporate planning itself needed to be planned properly. Ten areas of training were highlighted by Chakraborty (1983) keeping in view this perspective. He suggested scope for addition in the list of training programmes.

Saha and Datta (1983) recommended on-the-job training and off-the-job training in materials management. They predicted that in the 1980s the material managers, according to Saha and Datta, will have to work hand in hand with designers and planners. The materials management basic statistics was discussed by Saha and Datta and need for systematic development of basic statistics with knowledge of Government rules/procedures would be required for material managers in organizations.

Khandelwal (1983) in another paper discussed about existing arrangements of NIBM for managerial training in public sector banks and pointed out a lack of strategy for MD training in banks. He suggested various areas that must be included in MD training for public bank managers at different levels. He also proposed that individual banks should enlarge their training activities by establishing a staff college and provide orientation programmes, functional programmes, and integrated programmes in management skills through these staff colleges.

Rao (1983) agreed that public enterprises had the infrastructure to take developmental activities. They also had the social responsibilities to develop women. Considering the heavy investments made in public sector, she proposed to train women so as to enable them to play their role and contribute the efficient functioning. In the United States, legislations had been imposed since long to provide equal opportunity to women enterprises. Such legislations may be enforced in India also which would prove more useful in comparison to reservation for women.

A review of Training and Development Journal showed that legislations were enforced in the United States to safeguard women in enterprises against their undue exploitation in corporations. Legislations of this nature are also required to be enforced in the Indian context to act as sequel to exploitation of women in industries.

Dholakia (1983) regarded the scope of MD broader than merely a question of quantitative magnitude of training needs. It was also the problem of quality of efforts that were made in meeting those needs. Dholakia (1983) reported the findings of a study conducted by the United Nations that the cost benefit analysis ratio of investment in building up MD institutions for public enterprises was highly favourable. Dholakia argued that the process of MD in public enterprises extended beyond the training and related services offered by recognized MD institutions. In addition to formal training it also involved the selection of right kind of personnel, developmental orientation on part of supervisory authority, creating a climate conducive to introducing the required change in managerial practices, and appropriate planning for managerial succession in public enterprises.

Prakash (1983) illustrated necessity for MD training and opined that participants in MD training programmes should include workers also. Various training methods were enlisted and five categories for including different topics into training programmes were suggested on the basis of review of management literature. Based on this study Ramu (1983) presented a paper dealing with personnel management which considered various systems and procedures of personnel management, pre-requisites offered to employees. Results were discussed in terms of employment in public sectors, wage policy, workers' participation at board level, benefits from training programmes, income distribution and policies of the Government. It was proposed that considering these factors would facilitate formulations of realistic personnel management policies. Ramu (1983) evaluated public enterprises by systems approach and various analyses such as performance analysis, efficiency analysis, and effective analysis were discussed.

Pareek (1983) presented a systematic evaluation of "Travacube" model which was a conceptual model of training evaluation.

Kalra (1983) discussed the importance and applicability of case method and syndicates in MD training. Based on earlier findings, Kalra (1983) was of the view that syndicate methods of training assumed special importance in Indian culture in addition to case method which generally proved useful. He suggested that in the Indian context if the case method and syndicates could take care of cultural factors. He expressed the view that these methods could also prove very effective tools for management education and training.

Raghavachari (1983) reviewed management training process during the past quarter of a century and concluded that it was not satisfactory. He discussed the problem of lack of an educational policy for building up public enterprise managers manpower and suggested different aspects for formulation of policy for training of managers. He also discussed role of external training institutions and universities. He finally proposed for formulation of a national education policy for training of public enterprises managers and establishment of National Institute of Training for Public Enterprises.

Prakash (1983) discussed elsewhere the efficacy of vestibule training in public enterprises and considered the vestibule training as vital base for preserving the viability of promotion opportunities in autonomous public corporations and Government companies.

Ganguli (1983) reviewed the MD in public enterprises and cited cases of different public sector organizations. He pointed out that there was absence of proper MD in public sector and a lack of proper manpower planning. Ganguli (1983) emphasized on rapport of public sector with private sector to be built up and following an integrative approach for MD scheme.

Sharma (1983) analyzed on-the-job training as a method of MD and discussed development of the same job, rotation and job based development techniques. Role of supervisors on coaching was also discussed.

Minocha (1983) concluded on the basis of analytical studies that the determination training exercise was an essential prerequisite of training programme. It was, however, normally not conducted which results into a mis-matching of training and needs/expectations of trainees. The review of literature revealed that most of the methods for determining training needs in public enterprises turned to be informal, superficial, sporadic, subjective, and holistic rather than being formal, objective and particularistic. Minocha (1983) provided a diagnostic evaluation of the methods of determining training needs of public enterprises.

Handa (1983) emphasized on the importance of training to improve the capabilities of employees and contribute to the administrative capacity of the enterprise. He discussed training needs, objectives and methods for training in performance budgeting.

Singh and Pant (1983) designed a study to inquire into the problem of public enterprises as perceived by the public sector managerial community. They concluded that (a) the perceived problems of public enterprises were not significantly influenced by managerial age, hierarchy, experience, nature of industry, and organizational ability to generate surplus, (b) political interference and politicization of economic issues, instability at top, intervention by the concerned ministry, and union's interference made the managers helpless and deputation of people at top having no adequate and relevant experience of managing business organizations were viewed as critical factors that made the public enterprises ineffective, (c) managerial freedom and autonomy seemed to be completely eroded due to the interference of political parties, the concerned ministry, and unions. The process of control was with politicians and bureaucrats at the Centre, and not with the managers who were directly responsible for the operations of the public enterprises. Such an erosion of managerial power was bound to lead to helplessness, powerlessness, and consequent alienation, (d) there was no stability at the top which caused a lot of discontinuity in organizational policies and programmes, and (e) public enterprises were not managed by poor quality of people but poor management systems and processes and poor salary and perks were responsible for low performance of public enterprises.

Mishra and Ravishankar (1983) proposed designing and implementation of an OD and training strategy for public enterprises. Mishra and Ravishankar (1983) discussed the process of developing training system, method of evaluation of training programmes, and role of trainers.

Ravishankar and Mishra (1985) discussed needs of training, existing training system, some core problems pertaining to the existing training system, identification of training needs and objectives, and described the objectives of training for junior, middle and top/senior level managers' training groups. They also discussed about curriculum of training, methods of training, evaluation of results, and trainer effectiveness to emphasize the qualitative dimension in training need to be proved in-depth in the context of the varying needs for training of individual trainees and organizational requirements.

Warrier (1985) discussed about training of effectiveness leadership and various approaches and methods for leadership development/MD training for managers in public sector organizations.

Monappa (1985) conducted a study on 186 managers including a few female managers. The organizations included in the sample were from the public/private sectors, large multinationals to small scale units. Data analysis suggested seven broad areas of concern to line/service managers vis-a-vis the personnel function. The areas were: (a) structure location and autonomy of personnel department in the organization, (b) manpower planning and recruitment selection, (c) employee development and training, (d) working conditions, welfare and reward systems, (e) industrial relations, and (f) system procedure, and standards. Issues concerning the managers in each of the areas were discussed and solutions or desired approaches towards the solution to the problems were also discussed.

Kazmi (1985) conducted a study to investigate process of evaluation in management training through a questionnaire survey of management trainers. 146 trainers from 111 organizations were contacted and 43 of them responded from 36 public sector organizations. The survey was conducted from October, 1982 to February 1983. For the purpose of comparative analysis, the sample was divided into three groups, viz., public sector, private sector and autonomous training institutions. A part of the study dealt with the use of different training evaluation methods of management trainers theoretically. Sixteen evaluation methods were identified for the study. The results were discussed in terms of comparative analysis of evaluation methods. It was concluded that evaluation training in public sector organizations was done only in the form of immediate assessment during and after the training in terms of improved behaviour and performance were rarely measured rendering the evaluation exercise as somewhat superficial. Cost benefit analysis, though a difficult method of assessment and rigorous, yet needed to be adapted as an evaluation method. The autonomous training institutions used these methods, therefore, they may not be impracticable as they might seem to be.

From the above review of literature it is clear that most of the researches have been done in the area of training design, training methods, management development, models and theories, organizational development, job design and job aids. Indian studies have focussed on different aspects of conceptual framework for management development, functional areas, performance criteria and methodological issues, approaches and policies, need for management developing training, effectiveness of training and training evaluation. These studies facilitate further investigation in the unexplored area of personality characteristics and individual differences of managers that has bearing on formulating intervention strategies for management development on the basis of identified training needs of managers. Need based training has been thought of lately to make the training process more useful for those to be trained for their overall development. Need-based training will also facilitate planners of MD interventions and the trainers who have to contribute in the management and development process. In order to study the influence of some psychological correlates of MD training such as occupational aspiration, job involvement, quality of work life, motivating potential, job satisfaction, achievement value and background variables on perception of training experience of trainee managers of two organizations imparting them on-the-job training some hypotheses were developed. A description on development of hypotheses for the study is dealt in the following section.

SECTION II

4

DEVELOPMENT OF HYPOTHESIS

The present section deals with various hypothesis being developed for the study, the methodology followed for investigation and development of a measure for attitude towards training. In this chapter rationale for the hypothesis is discussed, which were framed to study the impact of psychological variables on training experiences.

The following paragraphs are devoted to highlight the relevance of Occupational Aspiration, Job Involvement, Quality of Work Life, Motivating Potential, Job Satisfaction, Achievement Value, and background variables in the present context of the study.

Hypothesis I

Occupational Aspiration refers to the ambition and need for professional growth and development through rise and promotion to top positions of management. This also refers to ambition for having increased capability, keenness to learn and improve knowledge and performance, being intelligent, skilled, talented, sincere to work and honesty and willingness for innovations for the organizational growth and development. These needs and ambitions for professional growth and development may be satisfied through training. Therefore, the perception of training experience is likely to be affected by Occupational Aspiration of the trainee.

Rabinowitz (1980) proposed a developmental model of Job Involvement (JI) and found some support for the additive effects theory of JI. The combination of variables was found to be significantly related to JI. This included participation in job training, personal orientation, reward expectancy, job satisfaction, job scope and socio-economic status.

Thus, it is clear that JI has been considered as an important variable in training experience. It was, therefore, hypothesized that:

H.1. Occupational Aspiration and Job Involvement were positively related to attitude towards training.

Hypothesis II

Mehtani (1985) conducted a study to find out the Work-Value Orientation of Indian students. Cross-cultural comparisons revealed that there were cultural differences in the work value orientation.

Another study related with work was conducted by Mohan and Jahangiri (1985) to analyse managerial effectiveness in relation to occupational goal values. It was observed that the intrinsic goal values did not seem to determine the effectiveness.

According to Sikula (1971) values and value systems were merely priority patterns along a continuum of importance. More insightful analysis of motivated behaviour can be made via the use of value concept. He further emphasised that the studies of values was a new and promising approach to explain motivated behaviour.

The value of an individual have bearing on his perceptions, it was, therefore, hypothesized that:

H.2. Achievement value was positively related to Attitude towards training.

Hypothesis III

Klien (1978) examined the Hackman-Oldham Job Enrichment theory using core job characteristics (skill, variety, task identity, task significance, autonomy and feedback) scale. The results provided only partial support for the theory.

Baker (1978) used six dimensions similar to Hackman and Oldham's Job Diagnostic Survey and suggested that some of the six dimensions of job content were not independent variables but that autonomy, value and feedback are sub-factors of job challenge (i.e. skill and variety).

Brousseau (1977) studied effects of job experience on personality and found that two personality characteristics: Orientation and freedom from depression were influenced by several job characteristics (of Hackman and Oldham Job Diagnostic Survey).

Walsh (1980) used a model categorizing job characteristics being fitted to data on three different samples and used a path analysis technique (LISREL). He reported that challenge consistently emerged as the primary determinant of job satisfaction, while the impact of role clarity varied from among the three samples. Role clarity appeared to be a necessary pre-condition for perceived challenge. Differences among the three samples suggested that the effect of job characteristics on individual outcomes might be contigent upon the organizational setting.

Since perception of job characteristics and training experience both might be explained through job enrichment concepts and provide Growth Needs and Motivating Potential, it was hypothesized that:

H.3. Motivating Potential score had positive relationship with Attitude towards Training.

Hypothesis IV

Job Satisfaction has been studied in relation to a number of variables, e.g., Srivastava (1985) studied job satisfaction among private and public sector employees with special reference to achievement motivation and found that private and public sector employees significantly differed in the level of Achievement Motivation and Job Satisfaction.

Rao and Ganguli (1972) studied Job Satisfaction of highly skilled personnel to test the generality of two-factor theory of Herzberg.

Pratap and Srivastava (1985) conducted a study to compare private and public sector textile industries in terms of Job Satisfaction and Organizational Climate. The study revealed that there was significant difference between private and public sector employees in terms of Job Satisfaction and Organizational Climate and the relationship between Job Satisfaction and Organizational Climate was also significant (r=.07), Srivastava (1985) studied job satisfaction among private and public sector employees who significantly differed in the level of Achievement Motivation and Job Satisfaction. Thus, it is clear from the above studies that Job Satisfaction affects other variables and is also, in turn, affected by other variables.

Carter conducted an exploratory study among worker groups on Quality of Work Life (QWL) and attempted to explore the worker's experience of work at its best and to consider what the conditions for the experience might be. The study showed that an experience of QWL occurred when the workers competence was being validated by three primary sources of information:

1. the impact of the work on the workers environments.
2. the extent to which the work was perceived by the worker to be self-determined, and
3. the degree of harmony experienced by the worker within work.

Cornel (1985) conducted a study to find out conditions which influence job performance and QWL. The results suggested that the efforts to improve QWL should center on organizational variables. It was also suggested that the workplace would be viewed as a multi-dimensional phenomenon in terms of both cause and effect.

Grady (1985) investigated the relationship between employee participation in Quality Circles and changes in their Work Life

Quality and productivity. Positive relationship between Quality Circle participation and changes in QWL perceptions were found in area directly involved in Quality Circles but not in more general work life areas. The results suggested that Quality Circle involvement acted more to provide social support to buffer participants from negative contextual factors than to enhance QWL. Organizational records were also assessed from six months before two to four months after adoption of the QC programme and showed that QC participation led to improvement in employee productivity and absenteeism

The afore mentioned studies reveal that perception of QWL largely affects the attitudes of individual and his performance/ productivity. It is, therefore, hypothesized that:

H.4. Job Satisfaction and Quality of Work Life were positively related to Attitude towards Training.

Hypothesis V

Relationship between an individual's demographic characteristics and responses to work environment had been investigated by Herman and Hulin (1972) who demonstrated that within the same organization demographic background accounted for a significant portion of variance in responses to work environment.

H.5. Background variables would show relationship with Attitude towards Training.

Hypothesis VI

Parmeswaran (1983) discussed the inter-relationship of psychological processes of perception, learning motivation and personal growth. These processes are influenced by each other. The psychological and individual variables, viz., Occupational Aspiration, Achievement Value, Job Involvement, perception of Quality of Work Life, Job Satisfaction and Motivation Potential are likely to affect the perception of Training Experience. It was, therefore, hypothesized that:

H.6. The Training Experience could be predicted by Occupational Aspiration, Job Involvement, QWL, J.S. (Job Satisfaction), M.P.S. (Motivating Potential Score), and Achievement Value.

The methodology to test the above mentioned hypothesis is dealt in the following chapter which gives a detailed account of sample, operational definitions of the variables, research instruments used for various measures and statistical analysis.

5

METHODOLOGY

The study had been conducted with survey research design which was thought to be appropriate to start research in the still unexplored area. The perceptual responses were obtained in order that the individual differences might also become evident from the survey. This chapter presents the description of sample, variables, operational definitions of the variables under reference, instruments used for data collection and statistical analysis.

Sample Selection and Sample Characteristics

Two organizations were selected on the purposive basis: (1) an Engineering Training Organisation, where Engineers were given on-the-job training, and (ii) a social welfare functionaries training organization imparting training to Social Welfare Officers. Both the organisations were in public sector. The respondents functioned as managers in their respective organizations. A sample of 130 Engineers was drawn from various training programmes in a particular year from the engineering organization and 170 Social Welfare Officers were included in the study from various training courses, participating in various training programmes in a particular period of time. All the trainees of those training programmes were included in the study from the engineering and social welfare training organization. Thus, the batches of trainees of a training programme constituted the sample. Since number of trainees differed in different training batches in both the organizations, the total number of trainees varied slightly (i.e. 130 and 170 respectively).

As it was a common characteristic of such training courses, the trainees constituting different batches of training programmes differed in age, educational background, experience, and family background. The sample characteristics for the two organisations were the following:

Organization I (Engineers)*

a.	Average age	3.13
b.	Average pay scale	3.00
c.	Average number of workers supervised directly	79.00
d.	Average educational level	2.95
e.	Average experience(in years)	7.28

* The average values were computed for a sample of 130 Engineers on the basis of categories worked out for the background information.

Organization II (Social Welfare Officers)*

a.	Average age	2.65
b.	Average pay scale	2.39
c.	Average number of workers supervised directly	16.08
d.	Average educational level	1.27
e.	Average experience	7.71

* The average values were computed for a sample of 170 SWOs on the basis of categories worked out for the background information.

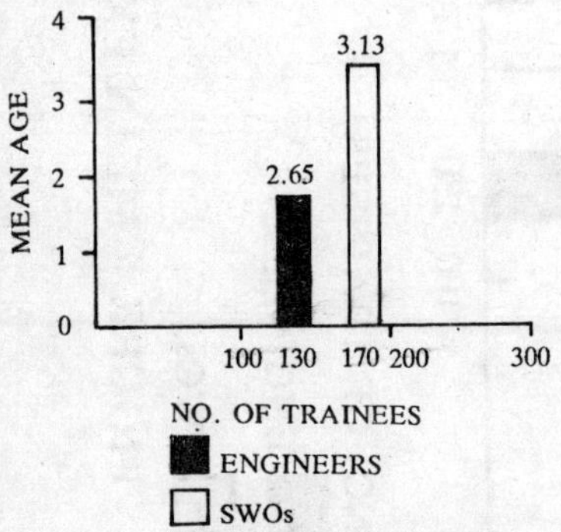

FIGURE 1. MEANAGE

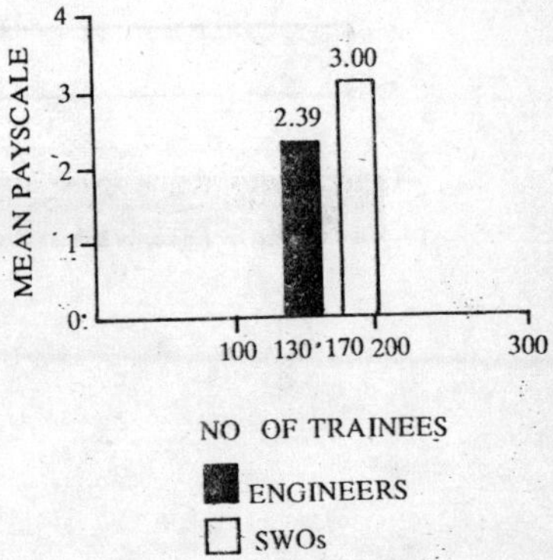

FIGURE 2. MEAN PAYSCALE

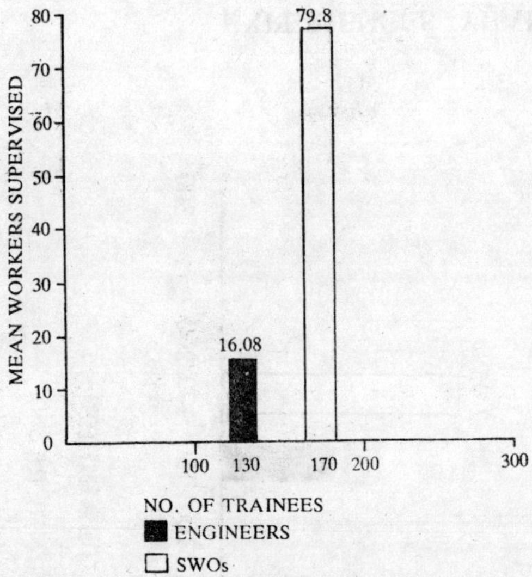

FIGURE 3. MEAN OF WORKERS SUPERVISED DIRECTLY

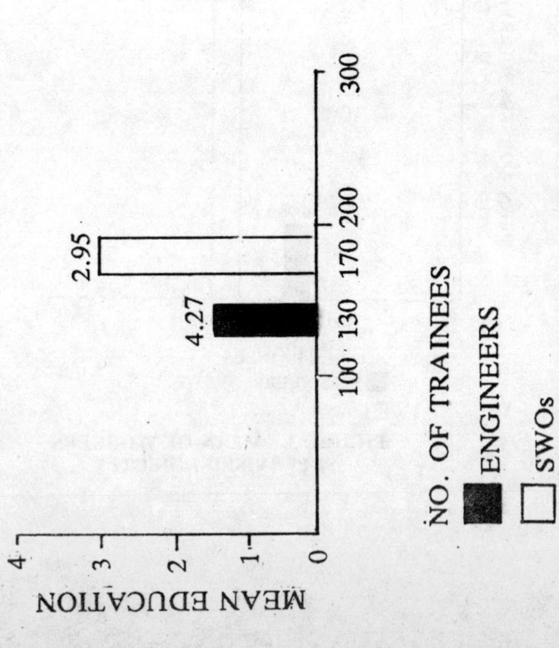

FIGURE 4. MEAN EDUCATION

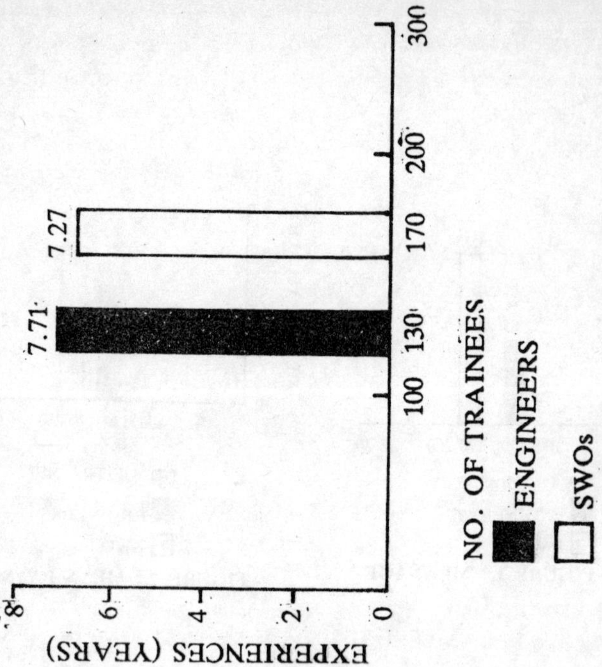

FIGURE 5. MEAN EXPERIENCE

The mean values for age, sex, pay scales, workers supervised, education, and experience as shown in the Figures 1, 2, 3, 4, and 5 respectively establish that on the whole the Engineers and SWOs differed on the various background variables. On every background variable variances/similarities have been discussed below.

(a) **Age**: Average age for Engineers sample was 3.13 as against Social Welfare Officers (SWOs sample for which the average age was 2.65). These averages show differences in the age group between the two samples (Figure 1).

(b) **Sex** : The Engineers sample comprised only males. On the contrary, among the SWOs both males and females constituted the sample. Thus, on this background variable the sample characteristics of the two samples were distinct.

(c) **Pay Scales** : Analysis of different pay scale categories for the two samples showed an average of 3.00 for Engineers and 2.39 for SWOs. Two different averages for the two samples clearly differentiated between the pay scales of the two organisations (Figure 2).

(d) **Workers Supervised** : The average number of workers being supervised directly by Engineers is just 16.08 in contrast to 79.43 by SWOs. Thus the average number of workers supervised distinctly varied between the two samples (Figure 3).

(e) **Educational Level** : The average educational level in case of Engineers was 2.95 as against 1.27 for SWOs. These results indicated difference between the two samples in the average educational level (Figure 4).

(f) **Experience** : Average on-the-job experience in case of Engineers was more than the social welfare officers, as shown in figure 5.

These results led to the conclusion that the two samples differed on the background variables and showed different characteristics, specially on the sex variable. On the other above-mentioned background variables also, the two samples had shown different characteristics which was indicative of the fact that there were distinct individual differences in the two samples as also among the trainees on the background variables under study.

Independent Variables: In the present study the following Independent Variables (IVs) had been investigated :

1. *Background Variables*

(a) Age, (b) Sex, (c) Pay Scale, (d) No. of workers supervised directly, (e) Educational level, and (f) Experience.

2. *Psychological Variables*

   a. Occupational Aspiration
   b. Job Involvement
   c. Quality of Work Life
   d. Motivating Potential
   e. Job Satisfaction
   f. Achievement Value.

Dependent Variables : The Dependent Variable was the perception of Training Experience.

Operational Definitions : For the purpose of this study the above mentioned variables had been defined operationally. The following were the operational definitions:

(i) Background Variables

The background variables included were those personal and profession related general informations which facilitated the understanding about individual trainee, i.e., age-group, sex, scale of pay, number of workers supervised directly, educational background and total experience on-the-job.

(ii) Occupational Aspiration

Occupational Aspiration referred to the ambition and need for professional growth and development. This also included promotion to top positions of management for having increased control and more responsibility. Thus, Occupational Aspiration included feeling of capability, being intelligent, skilled and talented, keenness to learn and improve knowledge and performance, sincerity to work, honesty and willingness for innovations for the organizational growth and 'development'.

(iii) Job Involvement

Job Involvement referred to individual's willingness to invest himself in pursuit of job activities. Highly involved person demonstrated a strong desire to be at work, willing to exert himself to cope with the demands of his job, and experienced his work as self-rewarding.

(iv) Quality of Work Life

Quality of Work Life might be defined as the degree to which members of work group organization were able to satisfy important personal needs through their experiences in the organization.

Perception of conduciveness of organization and its work environment for satisfaction of employee needs had been considered for the purposes of this study as the Quality of Work Life.

(v) Motivating Potential

Motivating Potential was defined as the degree to which a job had potential to motivate an individual to work in terms of skill and variety, task identity, task significance, autonomy, and feedback.

(vi) Job Satisfaction

The perception of the individual about need fulfilment opportunities according to his expectations might be operationally defined as Job Satisfaction.

(vii) Achievement Value

Operationally defined, the Achievement Value of an individual was the importance that he attached to a particular job activity or personal activity (including hobbies, personal social interaction, etc.), or any other activity.

(viii) Training Experience

Training Experience was the perception of the training process as a whole and the different specific aspects of the training process as a means of professional and personal growth, adjustment and development to gain knowledge and skills.

Instruments

In order to study the aforesaid independent and dependent variables the following research instruments had been used for collecting data:

1. Background Information Form
2. Occupational Aspiration Scale
3. Training Experience Questionnaire
4. Quality of Work Life Questionnaire
5. Motivating Potential Scale
6. Job Satisfaction Scale
7. Achievement Value Inventory.

Of these, the Background Information Form, Occupational Aspiration Scale, Training Experience Questionnaire, and Quality of Work Life Questionnaire had been developed by the author. Description of each of the instruments used for the study is given below followed by that of the data collection and analysis.

Description of Instruments

(a) **Background Information Form**: The background information form was developed to collect information on age, sex, scale of pay, department/section where the respondents worked in their organization, number of workers being supervised directly by the respondents, nature of educational level, and total experience in the present job.

(b) **Occupational Aspiration Inventory**: The Occupational Aspiration was measured by a Likert type inventory which comprised 33 items selected after pre-testing. Prior to pre-testing opinions of judges had been obtained. The items of the inventory were based on various aspects of Occupational Aspiration.

(c) **Training Experience Questionnaire**: In order to get responses on the perception of training experience, a Likert type questionnaire had been developed. The questionnaire consisted of

18 items. The questionnaire included items on perception of training process and particular aspects of training in terms of gain of knowledge, skills development through training, solutions for day-to-day problems being faced on the-job-content of training, and development of necessary qualities through training. Development of this factor analysed questionnaire is discussed in chapter 6.

(d) **Quality of Work Life Questionnaire** : The Quality of Work-Life had been measured by a developed questionnaire of the Likert type. The scale included aspects like esteem for the organization, opportunities for growth and professional skill development, perception of the working conditions, work environment, attitudes of the management, etc. This was a factor analyzed questionnaire.

(e) **Job Involvement Inventory** : The measure used for job involvement was the Indian adaptation of Lodahl and Kejner (1965), the Job Involvement Inventory (Agarwal, U.N.). The inventory had also been pre-tested alongwith developed instruments.

Reliability : The split-half reliability for the Phase V Sample (N=50) for the 32 items JI scale was computed by calculating the product moment correlation co-efficient between odd-even halves of the scale. Split-half correlation corrected by means of the Spearman Brown formula, was .85. Chronbacks (1951) co-efficient alpha for the Phase III Sample (N=214) was: .87.

In an attempt to shorten the JI scale, a least-square delete multiple regression was computed to order the scale items in terms of their ability to predict the 32-item JI scores. The 5-items scale explained about 80 per cent of the variance in the full scale. A 10 item version explained about 90 per cent of the variance in the full JI scale corrected split-half correlation (based on odd vs even-numbered items) for the 5 item scale was .57. So the 5 item scale could be uitlized to economize on respondent's time without much loss in precision but with considerable loss in reliability.

Validity : The 32-items JI scale possessed convergent validity and met the first and the fourth tests for discriminant validity.

Convergent Validity : Although the two JI convergent validity co-efficients (monotrait-hetro-method) of .33 and .21 were in expected direction, only the first was significantly different from zero.

Discriminant Validity

Test 1. The convergent validity co-efficients for JI (.33) was greater than the correlations lying in its column (-.03 and .11) and row (.21 and -.07) in the two appropriate hetro-trait hetro-method triangles.

Test 2. Evidence of discriminant validity was weak since the convergent validity co-efficients of .33 was greater than the hetro-traits hetro-method co-efficient of .00 but less than the co-efficient of .51.

Test 3. Discriminate validity was indicated by Kendall's co-efficients of concordance for the rank-order of inter-trait co-relations in the nine hetro-trait triangles (three mono-method, and six hetromethod). The computed S of 42 was less than the tabular S of 54 required for significance at the 5 per cent level.

Test 4. The corrected split-half reliability coefficients of the JI scale of .85 is greater than the hetro-trait-mono method co-efficients of .00, .51, .17.

Another evidence of the validity of the 32-item, JI scale was its correlation of .85 with Ladhal and Kejner's (1965) abbreviated JI scale, the Indian 5-item abbreviated scale correlated .59 Lodahl and Kejner's 5-item scale.

Construct Validity: A scale displayed construct validity if it was related to other variables as expected on the basis of past researches or theoretical considerations. The 32-items JI scale was related to the following variables for the sample of 322 managers:

1. Blood's(1969) Work Value Scale (r=.37;*P* <.01)
2. Rotter's (1966) External Control of Reinforcement(r=-.12; *P* <.05)
3. Work alienation (Pearlin, 1962) : (r=1; *P* < .01)
4. Lawler and Hall's (1970) Instrinsic Motivation Scale (r=.28; *P* <.1)

5. Sinha and Agarwala's (1971) Job Satisfaction Scale ($r = 1.20$; $P < .01$)

6. Self-defined Job Attractiveness (t for the difference in mean score for the first and fourth quartiles on job involvement was 3.56; $P < .01$)

7. Self-perceived Promotions Expectancy for 262 managers ($r = .15$, $P < .05$)

(i) 164 managers in Public Sector Firms ($r = .03$; not significant), and

(ii) 98 managers in private sector firms ($r = .35$, $P < .01$)

8. Technical and non-technical personnel (t for the difference in mean scores for the first and fourth quartiles on job involvement was 4.50; $P < .01$).

(f) **Motivating Potential Scale**: The measurement of motivating potential was done by using motivating potential measure based on Hackman-Oldham (1975) Job Diagnostic Survey. The Motivating Potential Score was measured on five job characteristics, viz., skill and variety, task identity, task significance, autonomy, and feedback was calculated by the relevant formula.

(g) **Job Satisfaction Scale** : Indresan's (1973) Job Satisfaction measure was used in this study. The scale was a Likert type, comprised 29 items and each one measured the different aspects of job satisfaction on a five-point scale.

(h) **Achievement Value Inventory**: Mukherjee's Achievement Value Inventory had been used to measure the Achievement Values in the present study.

Data Collection

The respondents were instructed to fill up the set of instruments provided to them. Each respondent was requested to give first frank reaction to each item. Rest pauses were allowed while the respondents gave their responses for different variables under investigation. Data was obtained on the above-mentioned questionnaires, inventories and scales for the Dependent and Independent variables in the classroom settings during the training programmes at the two training institutes for the two types of respondents.

Analysis:

The following statistical analysis were used for analysis of data collected from the respondents:

(a) Factor analysis of the Training Experience Questionnaire was computed;

(b) Correlation coefficients were computed to know the relationships between the criterion variable and independent variables;

(c) Multiple regression analysis had been computed to analyse the predictive value of independent variables;

(d) Both the samples (i.e. the Engineers and the Social Welfare Officers) had been analysed separately to find out mean difference between the two samples.

(e) Graphical representations were also included to show the trends, differences and characteristics of results.

The next chapter deals with discussion on development of scale for measuring the criterion variable of this study the Training Experience.

6

DEVELOPMENT OF SCALE

In this chapter development of the scale for measuring perception of training experience is described. The criterion variable, i.e., the training experience perception had been conceptualized through attitude towards training dimensions, which were included in the questionnaire and pre-testing was done to use the questionnaire for the measurement of criterion variable.

Attitude Towards Training Questionnaire: An attitude towards training questionnaire, a Likert type 5-point scale, was developed by the author to study the perception of training experience through attitude towards training. The questionnaire comprised of 18 items selected finally on the basis of pre-testing. The opinion of judges was obtained initially for selecting items. Based on the opinions of judges, items on which 75% or more judges agreed, were included and the questionnaire was pre-tested on Engineers receiving on-the-job training (N-60). The responses were obtained and items were subjected to inter-item correlation computation. Items with .50 and higher correlation. (Significant either at .01 or .05 level of significance) were drawn for inclusion in the questionnaire. Screen test was also used to finally draw the items for the questionnaire.

The following tables show the factor analysis for attitude towards training Table 3 and 5 show unrotated and rotated factors in case of Engineers, and Table 4 and 6 show unrotated factors for the other sample, i.e., Social Welfare Officers respectively.

TABLE 3

Unrotated Factor Matrix for Attitude towards Training

Item No.	*Factor.1 Training Effective-ness*	*Factor 2 Personal Growth & Develop-ment*	*Factor 3 Compe-tence*	*Factor 4 Gains from Training*	*Factor 5 Motivation for Personal Growth*
1.	-.47	.32	-.09	-.33	.33
2.	-.59	.11	.54	.08	.21
3.	-.60	.45	.34	.09	-.07
4.	-.55	.32	.28	.05	-.51
5.	-.49	.36	-.18	-.11	-.26
6.	-.70	.02	-.26	.42	-.07
7.	-.75	-.12	-.15	.31	.14
8.	-.72	.06	-.13	.21	-.30
9.	-.64	.21	-.38	-.21	-.12
10.	-.51	-.39	.08	-.03	-.10
11.	-.50	-.61	.07	-.01	.14
12.	-.74	-.22	-.08	.00	.18
13.	-.50	-.14	-.23	-.61	-.21
14.	-.47	-.03	-.59	-.31	.11
15.	-.41	-.56	.34	-.30	-.08
16.	-.48	-.52	.14	.19	-.00
17.	-.32	.31	.16	-.02	.54
18.	-.64	.28	.29	-.19	.03

N=130 (ENGINEERS)

TABLE 4

Varimax Rotated Factor Matrix for Attitude towards Training

Item No.	*Factor 1 Training Effective-ness*	*Factor 2 Personal Growth & Develop-ment*	*Factor 3 Compe-tence*	*Factor 4 Gains from Training*	*Factor 5 Motivation for Personal Growth and Development*
1.	-.03	.14	.14	.57	-.43
2.	.37	.12	.40	.59	-.21
3.	.05	.13	.67	.47	.07
4.	.10	.19	.83	.02	-.00
5.	-.10	.32	.49	.07	.36
6.	.20	.79	.24	.06	.05
7.	.39	.69	.12	.24	.07
8.	.25	.60	.48	-.02	.15
9.	.00	.71	.14	.25	.25
10.	.59	.20	.16	-.01	.13
11.	.76	.20	-.10	.08	.10
12.	.51	.45	.10	.30	.25
13.	.33	-.00	.26	-.02	.75
14.	.09	.38	-.09	.10	.71
15.	.79	-.18	.14	.03	.14
16.	.68	.28	.03	-.01	-.08
17.	-.03	.13	.01	.71	-.00
18.	.20	.11	.54	.49	.17

N = 130 (ENGINEERS)

Note : Items with a value of .50 and above were selected.

TABLE 5

Unrotated Factor Matrix for Attitude Towards Training

Item No.	*Factor 1 Training Effectiveness, Personal Growth and Development, Motivation for Personal Growth*	*Factor 2 Competence*	*Factor 3 Personal Growth and Development*
1.	-.41	-.73	.25
2.	-.44	-.76	.08
3.	-.52	-.69	-.07
4.	-.54	-.63	-.30
5.	-.52	-.59	-.35
6.	-.67	.15	.52
7.	-.79	.21	.40
8.	-.81	.27	.21
9.	-.81	.27	.14
10.	-.81	.23	-.02
11.	-.86	.18	-.04
12.	-.89	.21	-.15
13.	-.82	.23	-.29
14.	-.83	.22	-.28
15.	-.85	.17	-.20
16.	-.82	.18	-.26
17.	-.40	-.28	.61
18.	-.58	-.25	.12

N=170(SOCIAL WELFARE OFFICERS)

TABLE 6

Varimax Rotated Factor Matrix for Attitude towards Training

Item No.	*Factor 1 Training Effectiveness, Personal Growth and Development, Motivation for Personal Growth*	*Factor 2 Competence*	*Factor 3 Personal Growth and Development*
1.	-.04	.77	.40
2.	.03	.84	.25
3.	.17	.84	.14
4.	.28	.83	-.07
5.	.30	.80	-.12
6.	.47	.04	.72
7.	.64	.05	.66
8.	.74	.04	.48
9.	.76	.05	.42
10.	.79	.11	.27
11.	.82	.19	.27
12.	.89	.18	.17
13.	.89	.16	.01
14.	.89	.18	.03
15.	.86	.21	.11
16.	.85	.21	.05
17.	.03	.30	.73
18.	.35	.42	.33

N=170 (SOCIAL WELFARE OFFICERS)

Note : Item with a value of .50 and above were selected.

Tables 7 and 8 below reflect the Eigen values of each factors for the two samples followed by graphic representation of the Eigen values of the independent factors obtained after factor analysis. The graphic representation shows average Eigen values. The factors were extracted till the Eigen value reached 1.00.

TABLE 7

Eigen Values, Percentage of Variance and Cumulative Percentage of Factors

Sl. No.	*Name of Factors*	*Factor*	*Eigen Value*	*Percentage of Variance*	*Cumulative Percentage*
1.	Gains from Knowledge	4	5.91	32.8	32.8
2.	Gains from Knowledge	4	1.97	10.9	43.7
3.	Competence	3	1.44	8.1	51.8
4.	Competence	3	1.14	6.3	58.1
5.	Competence	3	1.04	5.8	.63.9
6.	Personal Growth & Development	2	0.96	5.4	69.3
7.	Personal Growth & Development	2	0.71	4.0	73.3
8.	Personal Growth & Development	2	0.71	4.0	77.3
9.	Personal Growth & Development	2	0.61	3.4	80.7
10.	Training Effectiveness	1	0.56	3.1	83.8
11.	Training Effectiveness	1	0.50	2.8	86.6
12.	Training Effectiveness	1	0.46	3.6	90.2
13.	Motivation for Personal Growth	5	0.40	2.2	92.4
14.	Motivation for Personal Growth	5	0.38	2.1	94.5
15.	Training Effectiveness	1	0.36	2.0	96.5
16.	Training Effectiveness	1	0.25	1.4	97.9
17.	Gains from Training	4	0.22	1.3	99.2
18.	Competence	3	0.15	0.8	100.0

N=130 (ENGINEERS)

TABLE 8

Eigen Values, Percentage and Variance and Cumulative Percentage of Factors

Sl. No.	*Name of Factors*	*Factor*	*Eigen Values*	*Percentage of Variance*	*Cumulative Percentage*
1.	Competence	2	9.06	50.3	50.3
2.	Competence	2	2.95	16.4	66.7
3.	Competence	2	1.48	8.2	74.9
4.	Competence	2	0.95	5.3	80.2
5.	Competence	2	0.80	4.5	84.7
6.	Personal Growth and Development	3	0.46	2.6	87.3
7.	Training Effectiveness, Personal Growth and Development	1	0.42	2.3	89.6
8.	Training Effectiveness, Personal Growth and Development	1	0.35	1.9	91.5
9.	Motivation for Personal Development	1	0.33	1.8	93.3
10	-do-	1	0.23	1.3	94.6
11.	-do-	1	0.20	1.1	95.7
12.	-do-	1	0.18	1.1	96.8
13.	-do-	1	0.15	0.9	97.6
14.	Training Effectiveness	1	0.13	0.8	98.4
15.	Personal Growth and Development	1	0.10	0.5	98.9
16.	-do-	1	0.08	0.4	99.3
17.	Motivation for Personal Growth	1	0.07	0.4	99.7
18.	-do-	1	0.05	0.3	100.0

N=170 (SOCIAL WELFARE OFFICERS)

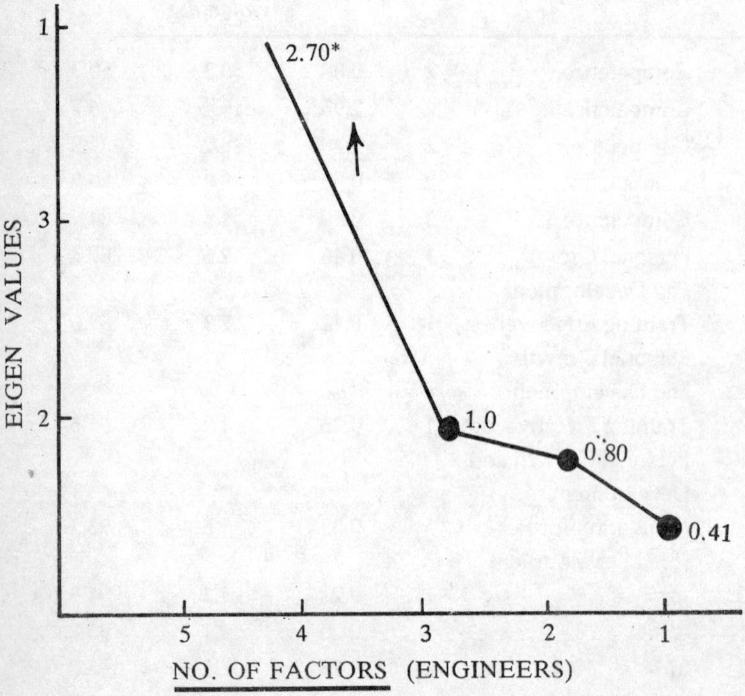

Eigen Values of Five independent Factors obtained after factor analysis.

The factors were extracted till the value reached 1.

* Average values.

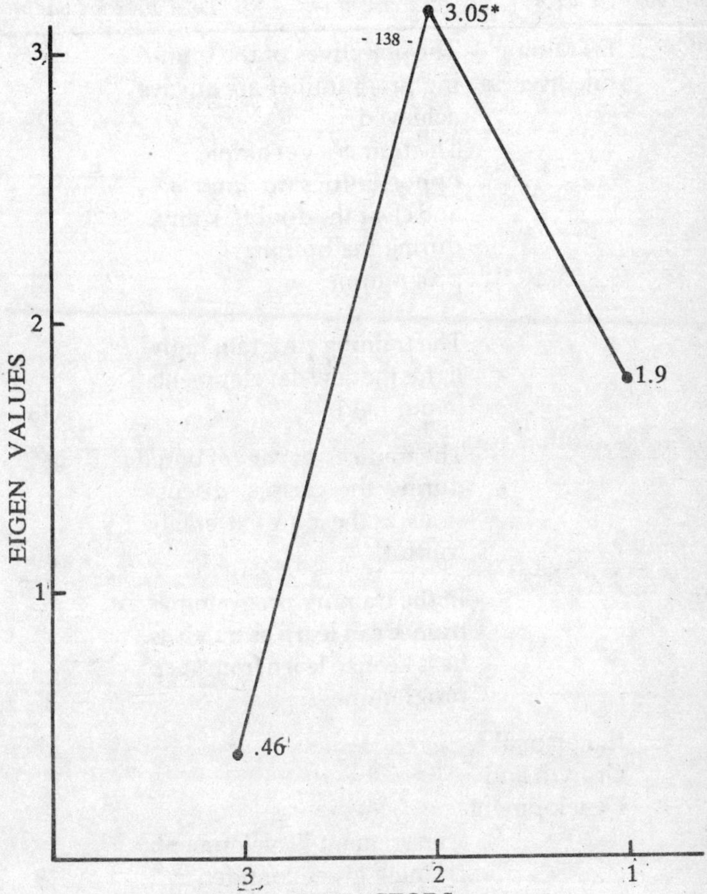

NO. OF FACTORS
(SOCIAL WELFARE OFFICERS)

Eigen Values of Three independent Factors obtained after factor analysis.

The factors were extracted till the value reached 1.

* Average values.

TABLE 9

Factor Scores; Dimensions of Training Experience

Item No.	*Factor*	*Statement*	*Factor Loading*
10.	I. Training Effectiveness	The objectives of the training programmes are always achieved.	.22
11.		The trainees get ample opportunities to improve and clear the doubts, if any, during the training programmes.	.31
12.		The training program highlights the new developments in our field	.13
15.		The trainees never get bored during the classes, discussions, as these are extremely fruitful.	.36
16.		In the training programmes a trainee can learn as much as he is keen to learn from such programmes.	.27
	II. Personal Growth and Development		
6.		Management Development Training gives confidence	.39
7.		This type of training gives latest knowledge	.30
8.		The training helps decision making	.23
9.		The basic idea in such training is clear to participant trainees as to what are the aims of the training programmes	.33

Item No.	*Factor*	*Statement*	*Factor Loading*
		aims of the training programs.	
4.		The content of the training programmes prepares us to face new challenge in decision making.	.25
5.		Inculcation of the value of responsibility and growth are the aims of such Management Development Training.	.24
	III. Personal Growth and Development		
6.		Management Development Training gives confidence	.35

N=170 (SOCIAL WELFARE OFFICERS)

TABLE 10

Factor Scores; Dimensions of Training Experience

Item No.	*Factor*	*Statement*	*Factor Loading*
	I. Training Effectiveness, Personal Growth and Development, motivation for Personal growth.		
7.		This type of training gives latest knowledge.	.02

Item No.	*Factor*	*Statement*	*Factor Loading*
8.		The training helps in decision making.	.07
9.		The basic idea in such training is clear to participant trainees as to what are the aims of training programmes.	.08
10.		The objectives of the training programmes are always achieved.	.11
11.		The trainees get ample opportunities to improve and clear the doubts, if any, during the training.	.11
12.		At least 80% trainees are keenly interested in the training.	.17
14.		The trainees never get bored during the classes, discussions as these are extremely fruitful.	.15
15.	II. Competence	In the training programmes a trainee can learn as much he is keen to learn from such programmes.	.16
1.		I get richer in knowledge and experience by the training that is imparted to managers here.	.21
2.		The technical training imparted to us in this organisation gives solution to many of the day-to-day problems.	.24
3.		Training here is job specific.	.24

Item No.	*Factor*	*Statement*	*Factor Loading*
3.	III.Competence	The training equips managers for various problem-solving situations.	.30
4.		The content of the training programmes prepares us to face new challenge in decision making.	.51
5.		Inculation of the value of responsibility and growth ment development training.	.24
18.		The training develops competence in handling various new and unusual situations.	.19
1.	IV. Gains from Training	I get richer in knowledge and experience by the training that is imparted to managers here.	.36
2.		The technical training imparted to us in this organisation gives solution to many of the day-to-day problems.	.33
17.		Training here is job specific.	.52
	V. Motivation for Personal Growth		
13.		At least 80% trainees are keenly interested in the training programmes.	.53
14.		The motivating factor in attending training programmes is the personal growth.	.46

N =130 (ENGINEERS)

Tables 11 and 12 below shows the transformation matrix of factor analysis of the Questionnaire for Engineers' and SWO's sample:

TABLE 11

Transformation Matrix

Sl. No.	Factors	Factor 1	Factor 2	Factor 3	Factor 4	Factor 5
1.	Training Effectiveness (1)	-.49	-.57	-.46	-.37	-.30
2.	Personal Growth and Development (2)	-.80	-.07	-.45	-.38	-.02
3.	Competence (3)	.33	-.52	.41	.33	-.58
4.	Gains from Trg. (4)	-.08	.63	-.08	-.15	-.75
5.	Motivation for Personal Growth (5)	.01	.04	-.64	.77	-.05

N = 130 (ENGINEERS)

TABLE 12

Transformation Matrix

Sl.No.	Factors	Factor 1	Factor 2	Factor 3
1.	Training Effectiveness, personal growth and development, motivation for personal growth	-.85	-.39	-.36
2.	Competence	.43	-.90	-.03
3.	Personal Growth and Development	-.31	-.17	.93

N=170 (SOCIAL WELFARE OFFICERS)

Tables 4 and 6 show the factor loading of items of the questionnaire.

Scoring : Each respondent was required to evaluate himself on a five-point scale ranging from 1 to 5 with regard to the degree to which he agreed with a particular statement of the scale. A composite score was obtained by adding score on each item. Items of the final questionnaire facilitated measurement of Attitude towards Training which was predictive of perception of Training Experience of the respondent trainees.

The following chapter comprises results of the study. The results have been discussed with reference to the hypothesis designed for the study. Each hypothesis was tested according to the results of the study.

[illegible] properties [illegible] [illegible] [illegible] [illegible] hypothesis [illegible] [illegible]

[illegible] each type [illegible] the result [illegible]

TABLE 13
Inter-Variable Correlations

SERIAL NO.	VARIABLES	BACKGROUND VARIABLE							QUALTIY OF WORK LIFE												TRAINING EXPERIENCE				
		Age	Pay Scale	No. of Workers Supervised Directly	Educational Level	Experience	Occupational Aspiration	Job Involvement	Organizational Image	Development Opportunities	Organizational Work	Motivating Work Climate	Insincerity	Organizational Strategies	Motivating Environment	Work Values	Demotivating Climate	Motivating Potential	Job Satisfaction	Achievement Value	Training Effectiveness	Personal Growth and Development	Competance	Gains from Training	Motivation for Personal Growth
1.	Background Variables																								
	a. Age	.00	.82*	.26*	.02	.34*	-.03	-.02	-.09	.06	.12	-.06	-.01	-.01	-.01	-.01	.12	.23*	-.05	.03	.06	-.26*	-.01	-.06	-.02
	b. Pay Scale	.82*	.00	.14	-.17**	.84*	-.00	-.07	-.03	.04	.21*	.02	-.04	-.00	.12	-.05	-.04	.31*	-.02	.09	-.10	-.36*	-.04	-.14	-.10
	c. No. of Workers Supervised Directly	.26	.14	.00	-.15	.24*	.03	-.10	-.13	-.08	-.09	-.17**	-.06	-.03	-.10	-.21**	-.18	-.10	-.11	-.17**	-.08	-.17**	-.20**	-.14	-.04
	d. Educational Level	.02	-.17**	.15	.00	.01	-.16**	.10	.16**	.18**	.16**	.04	-.03	.07	.09	.16**	-.00	-.11	.16**	-.09	.26*	.01	.05	.05	-.06
	e. Experience	.94*	.84*	.24*	.01	.00	.01	.01	-.05	.10	.16	-.04	-.03	-.03	.02	.01	.04	.26*	.02	.10	.05	-.28*	.02	-.03	-.07
2	Occupational Variation	-.03	-.00	.07	-.16**	.01	.00	.28*	.14	.13	.00	.28*	-.12	-.00	.01	.11	-.02	-.01	.12	.25*	.09	.31*	.24*	.23*	.28*
3.	Job Involvement	-.02	-.07	-.10	.10	.01	.03	.00	.20**	.14	-.07	.25*	.01	-.07	.00	.08	.13	-.00	.30*	.24*	.41*	.52*	.37*	.38*	.27*
4.	Quality of Work Life																								
	a. Organizationai Image	-.09	-.03	-.13	.16**	-.05	.14	.19**	.00	.61*	.39*	.65*	.04	.28*	.40*	.44*	-.39*	-.07	.31*	.06	.38*	.28*	.19**	.20**	.11
	b. Development Opportunities	.06	.04	-.08	.18**	.10	.13	.14	.61*	.00	.38*	.66*	.14	.19	.45*	.59*	-.36*	-.05	.26*	-.01	.47*	.23*	.20**	.25*	.22**
	c. Organizational Work Style	.17	.21**	-.09	.16**	.16**	.00	-.07	.39*	.38*	.00	.32*	.15	.16**	.32*	.36*	-.19**	.03	.19**	.08	.16**	-.03	.07	.17**	.01
	d. Motivating Work Climate	-.06	.02	-.17**	.04	-.04	.28*	.25*	.65*	.66*	.32*	.00	-.07	.14	.47*	.96*	-.31*	-.06	.38*	.11	.34*	.36*	.33*	.36*	.23*
	e. Insincerity	-.01	-.04	-.03	-.03	-.03	-.12	.01	.04	.14	.15	-.07	.00	-.08	.01	.16**	-.12	-.07	-.07	-.11	.19**	.13	.13	.01	.11
	f. Organizational Strategies	-.01	-.00	-.03	.07	-.03	-.00	-.07	.28*	.19**	.16**	.14	-.08	.00	.18**	.09	-.11	-.01	-.01	-.02	.14	.08	-.01	.13	.09
	g. Motivating Environment	-.01	.12	-.10	.09	.03	.01	.00	.40*	.45*	.38*	.47*	.01	.18**	.00	.54*	-.23*	.07	.23*	.12	.21**	.14	.27*	.28*	.32*
	h. Work Values	-.01	-.05	-.21**	.16**	.01	.11	.08	.44*	.59*	.36*	.50*	.16**	.08	.54*	.00	-.20**	-.05	.18**	.01	.28*	.13	.23*	.32*	.22**
	i Demotivating Climate	.12	-.04	.10	-.00	.04	-.02	.13	-.30*	-.36*	-.19**	-.31*	-.12	-.11	-.26*	-.28**	.00	-.08	-.20**	-.08	-.07	.09	.13	.08	-.14
5.	Motivating Potential	.23*	.31*	.10	-.11	.28*	.01	-.00	-.00	-.05	.03	-.06	-.07	-.01	.07	-.03	-.04	.00	.13	.12	-.17**	-.16**	-.01	.01	-.14
6.	Job Satisfaction	-.05	-.02	-.11	.16**	.02	.12	.30*	.31*	.26*	.14**	.35*	-.07	-.01	.24*	.18**	-.20**	.13	.00	.20**	.38*	.22**	.31*	.31*	.28*
7.	Achievement Value	.03	.09	-.17**	-.08	.10	.25*	.24*	.06	-.01	.08	.11	-.11	-.02	.12	.01	-.03	.12	.20**	.00	.16**	.16**	.19**	.16**	.09
8.	Training Experience (Attitude Towards Training)																								
	a. Training Effectiveness	.06	-.10	-.08	.86*	.05	.08	.41*	.38*	.47*	.16*	.34*	.20**	.14	.21**	.28**	-.07	-.17**	.38*	.16**	.00	.55*	.38*	.39*	.43*
	b. Personal Growth and Development	-.26*	-.36*	-.17**	.01	-.28*	.31*	.52*	.28*	.23*	-.03	.36*	.13	.08	.14	.13	.09	-.16**	.22**	.16**	.55*	.00	.60*	.51*	.45*
	c. Competence	-.01	-.04	-.20**	.05	.02	.24*	.37*	.19**	.20**	.07	.32*	.13	-.01	.27*	.23*	.13	-.01	.32*	.19**	.38*	.60*	.00	.62*	.38*
	d. Gains from Training	-.06	-.14	-.14	.05	-.03	.23*	.40*	.20**	.25*	.17**	.30*	.01	.13	.28*	.32*	.08	.01	.31*	.16**	.35*	.51*	.62*	.00	.29*
	e. Motivation for Personal Growth	-.08	-.10	-.04	-.06	-.07	.28*	.27*	.11	.22**	.01	.23*	.11	.09	.32*	.22**	-.14	-.14	.28*	.09	.43*	.45*	.39*	.29*	.00

N=130 (ENGINEERS) *P < .01 **P < .05

TABLE 14
Inter-Variable Correlations

SERIAL NO.	VARIABLES	BACKGROUND VARIABLE: Age	Sex	Pay Scale	No. of Workers Supervised Directly	Educational Level	Experience	Occupational Aspiration	Job Involvement	QUALTIY OF WORK LIFE: Motivating Work Climate	Development oppourtunity	Organizational Image and Strategies	Organisational Image and Fairness	Work Values	Insincerity	Organisational Strategies	Motivating Potential	Job Satisfaction	Achievement Value	TRAINING EXPERIENCE: Training Effectiveness Personal Growth and Development Motivation for Personal Growth	Competance	Personal Growth & Development
1.	Background Variables																					
	a. Age	.00	-.20**	.12	.04	-.27*	.80*	.02	.02	.04	-.01	.15	.04	.10	.12	-.01	.05	-.00	.08	-.06	.11	.11
	b. Sex	-.20**	.00	-.48*	-.11	-.13	-.12	.05	.11	.10	-.00	-.04	-.09	.11	.18**	.10	-.19**	-.00	.04	.13	.20**	.13
	c. Pay Scale	.12	-.48*	.00	.87*	.21*	.14	-.17**	-.12	-.08	-.04	-.23*	.02	.23*	-.17**	-.11	.27*	.17**	-.02	-.18**	-.20**	.16**
	d. No. of Workers Supervised Directly	.04	-.11	.37*	.00	.07	.13	-.03	.05	.01	.04	.00	.02	.05	-.03	-.00	-.01	-.00	.06	.06	.03	-.05
	e. Educational Level	-.27*	-.13	.21*	.07	.00	-.26*	-.16**	-.10**	-.02	-.07	-.21*	-.07	-.18**	-.18**	-.12	.15	.16	.08	-.17**	-.34*	-.32*
	f. Experience	.80*	-.12	.14	.13	-.26*	.00	-.05	.04	.09	.01	.10	.05	.05	.09	.00	.08	-.03	.01	-.02	.15	.04
2	Occupational Aspiration	.02	-.05	-.17**	-.03	-.16**	-.05	.00	.49*	.36*	.41*	.43*	.39*	.31*	.31*	.39*	-.47*	-.43*	-.13	.46*	.37*	.28*
3.	Job Involvement	.02	.11	-.12	.05	-.17**	.04	.49*	.00	.28*	.36*	.38*	.27*	.41*	.27*	.28*	-.46*	-.47*	.03	.37*	.40*	.27*
4.	Quality of Work Life																					
	a. Work Climate	.04	.10	-.08	.01	-.02	.09	.36	.29	.00	.16	.34	.30	.28	.28	.31	-.28	-.38	-.19	.25	.26	.11
	b. Development Opportunities	-.01	.00	-.04	-.04	-.07	.01	.41*	.36*	.16**	.00	.31*	.52*	.25*	.28*	.41*	-.37*	-.20*	-.57*	.47*	.23*	.39*
	c. Organizational Image and Strategies	.15	-.04	-.24*	.00	-.21**	.10	.43*	.38*	.34*	.31*	.00	.24*	.48*	.21*	.33*	-.42*	-.47*	-.02	.28*	.43*	.36*
	d. Organizational Image and Fairness	.04	-.04	.02	.02	-.07	.05	.39*	.27*	.30*	.52*	.24*	.00	.28*	.33*	.57*	-.40*	-.18**	-.08	.47*	.16**	.35*
	e. Work Value	.01	.11	-.23*	.05	-.19**	.05	.31*	.41*	.28*	.25*	.48*	.23	.00	.21*	.24*	-.39*	-.38*	.05	.33*	.42*	.32*
	f. Insincerity	.12	.18**	.17**	-.03	-.18**	.08	.31*	.27*	.23*	.29*	.21*	.33*	.21*	.00	.29*	-.63*	-.18**	.06	.31*	.21*	.49*
	g. Organizational Strategies	-.01	.10	-.11	-.00	-.12	.00	.39*	.29*	.21*	.41*	.32*	.37*	.24*	.49*	.00	-.64*	-.18**	.18**	.42*	.21*	.47*
5.	Motivating Potential	.05	-.18**	.22*	-.01	.15	.08	-.47*	-.46*	-.28	-.37*	-.42*	-.40*	-.39*	-.33*	-.64*	.00	-.36*	.14	-.54*	-.33*	-.44*
6.	Job Satisfaction	-.06	-.06	.17**	-.00	.16**	-.03	-.43*	-.47*	-.38*	-.20*	-.47*	-.18*	-.38*	-.15**	-.18**	.36*	.00	.07	-.27*	-.30*	-.04
7.	Achievement Value	.08	.04	-.02	.06	.08	.01	-.13	.02	-.19**	-.06	-.02	-.08	.05	.06	-.18**	-.14	.07	.00	.01	-.01	.10**
8.	Training Experience (Attitude Towards Training)																					
	a. Training Effectiveness Personal Growth and Development, Motivation and Personal Growth	-.05	.18	-.18**	.00	-.17**	-.02	.46*	.37*	.25*	.47*	.28*	.47*	.33*	.31*	.42*	-.54*	-.27*	.01	.00	.34*	.56*
	b. Competence	.11	.02	-.20**	.03	-.34	.15	.37*	.40*	.26*	.25*	.43*	.16**	.42*	.31*	.24*	-.53*	-.35*	-.12	.34*	.00	.24*
c.	Personal Growth and Development	.11	.13	-.16	-.05	-.32*	.04	.28*	.27*	.11	.38*	.26*	.35*	.32*	.49*	.47*	-.44*	-.04	.16*	.56*	.24*	.00

N=170 (SOCIAL WELFARE OFFICERS) * P < .01 **P < .05

SECTION III

7

RESULTS AND DISCUSSION

This chapter is devoted to present the results of the study and discussion on results obtained separately for the two samples. The investigation had aimed at studying some psychological correlates of training experience. The sample consisted of managers who received training in two different organizations. The two sets of datas for the two samples were analysed separately. Data had been analysed by using univariate, bivariate, and multivariate statistical methods. Product Moment Correlation Co-efficient was used to find out the relationship among the independent variables and the dependent variable. Regression analysis was computed to investigate the predictive power of independent variables. Factor analysis had been employed for development of questionnaires and to discuss the pattern of loadings for the two samples under study. Group means had also been analysed.

With the above mentioned brief description of the statistical analyses, a systematic account of the analyses employed and the results of the study for the two samples are discussed below. Each of the hypothesis have been tested in the light of results computed for the study. The first hypothesis was concerning the variables Occupational Aspiration and Job Involvement. Tables 13 and 14 show the relationship of all the variables with one another and gives a composite picture of inter-variable correlations found by analysis of data.

(i) **Engineers** : In case of Engineers, as Table 15 shows, Occupational Aspiration had significant correlation with "personal growth and development" (r=31, *P* < .01), "Competence" (r=.24, *P* < .01), "gains from Training" (r=.23, *P* <.01), and motivation for personal growth" (r=.28, *P* < .01). Occupational Aspiration had no relationship with "training effectiveness". Thus, except training effectiveness factor of Attitude towards Training, Occupational Aspiration showed positive significant relationship with the Attitude towards Training for the Engineers.

As regards Job Involvement, results have been shown in Table 15, which shows that Job Involvement had positive significant correlation with "training effectiveness" (r=.41, *P*. < 01)' "personal growth and development" (r=.52 *P* < .01), "Competence" (r=.37, *P*, < .01)' "gains from training" (r=.38, *P* < .01) and "motivation for personal growth and development" (r=.27, *P* < .01). It is evident that Job Involvement showed positive and significant relationship with Attitude towards Training.

(ii) **Social Welfare Officers:** In respect of the Social Welfare Officers (SWOs) Table 16 shows the results for the two variables and their relationship with the Dependent Variable, i.e., Attitude towards Training. As may be seen in Table 16, the Occupational Aspiration had significant correlation with "training effectiveness, personal growth and development", "motivation for personal growth" factor (r=.46, *P* < .01), with "Competence" (r=.37, *P* < .01). and with "Personal growth and development" (r=.28, *P* < .01).

(a) Occupational Aspiration

In both the samples, except the "training effectiveness", the other components of Attitude towards Training had significant correlation with Occupational Aspiration. However, the SWO's sample "training effectiveness", had not emerged as an exclusive component and was combined with "personal growth and development", and "motivation for personal growth". It may be said that due to motivation for personal growth Occupational Aspiration showed significant relationship. It may, therefore, be concluded that Occupational Aspiration did not substantially relate with training effectiveness.

TABLE 15

Correlation of Occupational Aspiration and Job Involvement with Attitude towards Training

Variables	*Occupational Aspiration*	*Job Involvement*
Attitude Towards Training		
(a) Training Effectiveness	.09	.41*
(b) Personal Growth and Development	.31*	.52*
(c) Competence	.24*	.37*
(d) Gains from Training	.23*	.38*
(e) Motivation for Personal Growth	.28*	.27*

N = 130

(Engineers) *P <.01

As shown in Table 16 Job Involvement related "training effectiveness, personal growth and development, motivation for personal growth" (r=.37 P <.01), with "Competence" (r=.40, P < .10), and "personal growth and development" (r=.26, P < .01)

TABLE 16

Correlation of Occupational Aspiration and Job Involvement with Attitude towards Training

Variables	*Occupational Aspiration*	*Job Involvement*
Attitude Towards Training		
(a) Training effectiveness, personal growth and development, motivation for personal growth	.46*	.37*
(b) Competence	.37*	.40*
(c) Personal Growth and Development	.28*	.26*

N = 170 (170)

(SWOs) *P <.01

Except the relationship of Occupational Aspiration with training effectiveness", the significant positive correlation with the rest components of Attitude towards Training supported the hypothesis that the Occupational Aspiration and positive relation with Attitude towards Training. Hence, first part of hypothesis 1 was retained.

(b) Job Involvement

The high positive correlation of Job Involvement supported the hypothesis. It was, therefore, concluded that Job Involvement had positive relation with Attitude towards Training. Hence second part of Hypothesis 1 was also retained.

Thus, Hypothesis 1 was supported by the results and findings confirm that these two variables, i.e., Occupational Aspiration and Job Involvement do have a relation and effect on the Attitude towards Training.

Hypothesis 2: Achievement Value is positively related to Attitude towards Training.

The above hypothesis was tested by the results in the following manner:

(i) Engineers

Results in Table 17 show that Achievement Value has significant Correlation with "training experience (r =.16 *P* < .05), "personal growth and development" (r=.16, *P* < .05) and "Competence" (r=.19, *P* < 05). Achievement Value, however, did not relate to "motivation for personal growth, as shown in Table 17.

(ii) SWOs

Achievement Value had significant correlation with only personal growth and development (r=.16, *P* < .05). Thus, the relationship between Achievement Value and Attitude towards Training was not established for the SWOs.

A clear distinction between the two samples was evident on this variable and, as the results showed, this variable did not link with the dependent variable in case of SWOs and the Engineers sample showed a just significant relationship in respect of "training effectiveness", "personal growth and development" and "gains from training". A higher correlation of the Achievement Value with "Competence" may be seen in Table 17 (Engineers) and in contrast to that for SWOs (Table 18).

The hypothesis was, thus, partially supported in case of Engineers and rejected for SWOs. Achievement Value, therefore, did not show a clear relationship with Attitude towards Training. Nevertheless it may be said that Achievement Value for managers in different types of organizations may appear as a correlate for Attitude towards Training. Further investigation is, therefore, required to verify beyond doubts if a relationship appears in different organizations.

TABLE 17

Correlation of Achievement Value with Attitude towards Training

Variables	*Achievement Value*
Attitude towards Training	
(a) Training Effectiveness	.16*
(b) Personal Growth and Development	.16*
(c) Competence	.19*
(d) Gains from Training	.16*
(e) Motivation for Personal Growth	.09*

N = 130

(ENGINEERS) *$P < .05$

TABLE 18

Correlation of Achievement Value with Attitude towards Training

Variables	*Achievement Value*
Attitude towards Training	
(a) Training effectiveness, personal growth and development, motivation for personal growth and development.	.01
(b) Competence	-.01
(c) Personal Growth and Development	.16*

N = 170

(SWOs) *$P < .05$

However, finding of the present study in respect of the relationship of Achievement Value with Attitude towards Training clearly shows that the respondent managers did not perceive that in their respective organizations training has anything to do for their growth and development. Rewards like appreciation for achievements increment in pay, recognition, fulfilment of psychological needs have no value in the public sector organizations. On the other hand, need for achievement is not encouraged in public sector, therefore, level of motivation to work would also be lowered. The public sector organizations seriously lack this important factor which takes a heavy toll on the overall performance in such enterprises. Resultantly heavy losses, low productivity, no motivation to work are the problems which are rampant in the public sector organizations. It was, therefore, thought to be appropriate to investigate effect of the motivating potential offered by the job on the attitude towards training. The third Hypothesis is pertaining to this highly important variable.

Hypothesis 3 : Motivating potential shows significant relationship with Attitude towards Training.

(i) **Engineers:** The results for Engineers sample showed that there was a significant negative relationship of Motivating potential with Attitude towards Training, particularly in relation to "training effectiveness" ($r=.17$, $P < .05$), and "personal growth and development" ($r = .16$, $P < .05$ (Table 19).

(ii) **SWOs:** So far as the other sample is concerned, motivating potential showed a high negatively significant relationship with "training effectiveness, personal growth and development, motivation for personal growth "— ($r = -.54$, $P < .01$) and $r = .44$, $P < .01$ respectively. "Competence ($r = -.33$, $P < .01$). The relationships are shown in Table 20.

These findings suggest that Attitude towards Training was not affected by Motivating Potential. The Motivating Potential did not positively influence the Attitude towards Training. On the contrary a negative correlation led to the inference that if the job had no motivating potential the individual would not have a need for enhancement in knowledge and skill. This perception of the individual strongly supports the fact that individuals are not

TABLE 19

Correlation of Motivating Potential with Attitude towards Training

Variables	*Motivating Potential*
Attitude towards Training	
(a) Training Effectiveness	-.17*
(b) Personal Growth and Development	-.16*
(c) Competence	-.01
(d) Gains from Training	.01
(e) Motivation for Personal Growth	-.14

N = 130 (ENGINEERS) *$P < .05$

TABLE 20

Correlation of Motivating Potential with Attitude towards Training

Variables	*Motivating Potential*
Attitude towards Training	
(a) Training effectiveness, Personal growth and development, motivation for personal growth and development.	-.54*
(b) Competence	-.33*
(c) Personal Growth and Development	-.44*

N = 170

(SWOs) *$P < .01$

motivated for training if the job does not have the five job characteristics in it (i.e., skill and variety, task identity, task significance, autonomy, and feedback) and the Growth Need Strength is weak. Thus, in the Indian conditions these job characteristics and Growth

Need Strength hold good, and more so among the managers in Indian public sector organizations. These conclusions are in congruence with Singh and Pant (1983) who designed a study to inquire into the problems of public enterprises as perceived by the public sector managerial community and concluded that (a) the perceived problems of public enterprises were not significantly influenced by managerial age, hierarchy, experience, nature of industry, and organizational ability to generate surplus, (b) political interference and politicization of economic issues, instability at top, intervention by the concerned ministry, and union's interference made the managers helpless, and deputation of people at top having no adequate and relevant experience of managing business organization have been viewed as critical factors that made the public enterprises ineffective (c) managerial freedom and autonomy seemed to be completely eroded due to the interference of political parties, the concerned ministry, and unions. The process of control was with politicians and bureaucrats at the Centre, and not with managers who were directly responsible for the operations of the public enterprise. Such an erosion of managerial power was bound to lead to helplessness, powerlessness, and consequent alienation, (d) there was no stability at the top which caused a lot of discontinuity in organizational policies and programmes, and (e) public enterprises were not managed by poor quality of people but poor management systems and processes and poor salary and perks were responsible for low performance of public enterprises.

The results in Tables 19 and 20 are also clearly indicative of the fact that among the managers in public sector organizations it is deep seated in their minds that the jobs which they are performing have no potential to motivate them; rather the jobs have proved to be demotivating. Therefore, any type or any amount of training for them is just a futile effort which would not alleviate them from the situations they are experiencing on their job. Thus, their jobs and working conditions demotivated the public sector managers selected for the study to the extent that they found no use of training for them irrespective of how useful training efforts were made to facilitate their competence, personal growth and development as well as professional development. Serious attention, therefore, is called for to improve the situation in the public sector organizations for the managers. The findings also suggested that when the job was not enriched, lesser need for training was felt by the individuals. But at the same time, further personal growth and development is a continuous process, and momentarily an individual may not perceive need for personal growth and development, still with advancement in technology and science, demand for training persists. It is, therefore, need of the time that innovations and advanced technology is introduced to modernize the plants and at the same time training is imparted to equip the managers with necessary knowledge and skills. On the other hand job enrichment may be implemented and more autonomy be allowed to effectively facilitate the managers, the top management and the Government to solve various problems being faced in the non-profit making or sick units/enterprises in the public sector. Among all these strategies the process of training would be helpful in increasing motivation level of managers who, in turn, would serve as 'change agents' within the organization to improve the existing situations to reduce heavy investments and heavy losses in the 'sick' public enterprises.

Hypothesis 4: Job Satisfaction and Quality of Work Life are directly related to Attitude towards Training.

(i) Engineers:

Job satisfaction showed high positive significant correlation with (a) training effectiveness (r=.38, $P < .01$), (b) Personal growth and development (r=.22, $P < .05$), (c) Competence (r=.32, $P < .01$), (d) gains from training (r=.31, $P < .01$), and (e) motivation for personal growth (r=.28, $P < .01$) These relationships are shown in Table 21. Further perusal of Table 21 reveals that the quality of work life has positive relationship with Attitude towards Training. Factor wise analysis shows the following:

(a) **Organizational Image:** Organizational Image had significant relationship with training effectiveness (r=.38, $P < .01$), Personal growth and development (r=.28, $P < .01$), Competence (r=.19, $P < .05$), gains from training (r=.20, $P < .05$), and no significant relationship with motivation for personal growth.

(b) **Development Opportunities:** Development Opportunities significantly, related to training effectiveness (r=.47, $P < .01$), personal growth and development (r=.23, $P < .01$), competence (r=.20, $P < .05$), gains from training (r=.25, $P < .01$), and motivation for personal growth (r=.22, $P < .01$).

(c) **Organizational Work Style** : Organizational work style had significant positive relationship only with (a) training effectiveness (r=.16 $P < .05$), and (b) gains from training (r =.17, $P < .05$).

(d) **Motivating Work Climate** : Motivating Work Climate had significant correlation with training effectiveness (r=.34, $P < .01$). personal growth and development (r =.36, $P < .01$), competence (r=.33, p < .01) gains from training (r=.30 $P < .01$) and motivation for personal growth (r=.23, $P < .01$). All the relationships were strongly positive as may be seen in Table 21.

TABLE 21

Correlation of Job Satisfaction and Quality of Work Life with Attitude towards Training

Variables	*Job Satisfaction*	*Quality of Work Life*								
		1	*2*	*3*	*4*	*5*	*6*	*7*	*8*	*9*
Attitude towards Training										
(a) Training Effectiveness	.38*	.38*	.47*	.16**	.34*	.19**	.14	.21**	.28*	-.07
b) Personal Growth and Development	.22*	.28*	.23*	-.03	.36*	.13	.08	.14	.13	.09
(c) Competence	.32*	.19**	.20**	.07	.33*	.13	-.01	.27*	.23*	.13
(d) Gains from Trg.	.31*	.20**	.25*	.17**	.30*	.01	.13	.28*	.32*	.08
(e) Motivation for Personal Growth	.28*	.11	.22**	.01	.23*	.11	.09	.32*	.22*	-.14

N = 130 (Engineers) *$P < .01$; *$P < .05$

Quality of Work Life

1. Organizational Image
2. Development Opportunities
3. Organizational Work Style
4. Motivating Work Climate
5. Insincerity

6. Organizational Strategies
7. Motivating Environment
8. Work Values
9. Demotivating Climate

(e) **Insincerity**: Insincerity related only with training effectiveness, as may be seen in Table 21.

(f) **Organizational Strategies**: Organizational strategies did not significantly relate to the 5 variables under the Attitude towards Training.

(g) **Motivating Environment**: Motivating Environment, as shown in Table 21, related to training effectiveness (r=.21, $P < .05$), Competence (r=.27, $P < .01$), gains from training (r=.28, $P < .01$), and motivation for personal growth and development (r=.32, $P < .01$).

(h) **Work Values** : Work values had correlation with training effectiveness (r=.28, $P < .01$), Competence (r=.23, $P < .01$), gains from training (r=.32, $P < .01$), and motivation for personal growth (r=.22, $P < .05$).

(i) Demotivating Climate:

The factor Demotivating Climate had no relationship with the variables under Attitude towards Training, as shown in Table 21.

(ii) Social Welfare Officers:

Table 22 shows that the job satisfaction negatively related to 'training effectiveness, personal growth and development, motivation for personal growth' and was significantly correlated with competence. Table 22 also shows that the Quality of Work Life generally had positive correlation with Attitude towards Training. Further study of Table 22 offers detailed findings, which are the following:

(a) **Motivating Work Climate**: Motivating Work Climate related with training effectiveness, personal growth and development, motivation for personal growth (r=-.27, $P < .01$), and there was positive correlation with competence (r=.35, $P < .01$).

TABLE 22

Correlation of Job Satisfaction, Quality of Work Life and Attitude towards Training

Variables	*Job Satisfaction*	*Quality of Work Life* 1	2	3	4	5	6	7
Attitude towards Training								
(a) Training Effectiveness, Personal Growth and Development, Motivation for Personal Growth.	-.27*	.25*	.50*	.30*	.50*	.33*	.31*	.42*
(b) Competence	-.35*	.30*	.23*	.43*	.16*	.42*	.21*	.21*
(c) Personal Growth and Development	.04	.26*	.11	.40*	.26*	.35*	.32*	.50*

N = 170 (SWOs) *$P < .01$

Quality of Work Life

1. Motivating Work Climate
2. Developmental Opportunities
3. Organizational Image and Strategies
4. Organizational Image and Fairness
5. Work Values
6. Insincerity
7. Organizational Strategies.

(b) **Developmental Opportunities**: Developmental opportunities had positive correlation with the three variables of Attitude towards Training, viz., training effectiveness, personal growth and development (r=.25, P<.01), competence (r=.30, $P < .01$), and personal growth and development (r=.26, $P < .01$).

(c) **Organizational Image and Strategies** : Organizational Image and Strategies showed relationship with training effectiveness, personal growth and development (r=.30, *P* < .01), competence (r=.43, *P* < .01), and personal growth and development (r=.40, *P* < .01) (Table 22).

(d) **Organizational Image and Fairness** : Organizational Image and Fairness, (as shown in Table 22) also related with training effectiveness, personal growth and development, motivation for personal growth (r=.50, *P* < .01), competence (r=.16, *P* < .05), and personal growth and development (r=.26, *P* < .01).

(e) **Work Values** : Work values also positively correlated with training effectiveness, personal growth and development, and motivation for personal growth (r=.33, *P* < .01), competence (r=.42, *P* < .01), and personal growth and development (r=.35, *P* < .01).

(f) **Insincerity** : Insincerity factor in case of SWOs related with training effectiveness, personal growth and development, motivation for personal growth (r=.31, *P* < .01), competence (r=.21, *P* < .01). and personal growth and development (r=.32, *P* < .01).

(g) **Organizational Strategies** : Organizational strategies are positively correlated with training effectiveness, personal growth and development, motivation for personal growth (r=.42, *P* < .01), competence (r=.21, *P* < .01), and personal growth and development (r=.50, *P* < .01).

The overall relationship of the QWL for Engineers emerged to be largely related with the ATT, whereas in case of SWOs the QWL highly related with ATT variables and strongly support the Hypothesis 4. Thus, the second part of the hypothesis that QWL is directly related to Attitude towards Training is retained for Engineers and strongly supported for SWOs sample.

The analysis of Table 21 reveals that Job Satisfaction is highly related with Attitude towards Training (ATT) for Engineers and these findings support the hypothesis. On the contrary, Job Satisfaction is negatively related to one variable of ATT and positively with another. Thus, partial support was shown by the findings for SWOs to the Hypothesis 4 with respect to relationship of job satisfaction and ATT. It is evident from the findings that Job Satisfaction for the Engineers' sample had influence on Attitude towards Training which in turn, leads to the conclusion that training was perceived as a means of enhancement in knowledge and skills on one hand, and on the other, training was perceived to be conducive to further increase in the job satisfaction. The other sample, i.e., SWOs perceived training not only to have an effect on their satisfaction from job but also non-conducive to their Job Satisfaction. The contradiction in the results for the two samples shows that the Engineers found their job satisfying even before coming to the training situation whereas the SWOs had not perceived their job as satisfying prior to entry in the training situation. Moreover, they perceived no role of training to be operative so far as satisfaction from the job was concerned.

These findings highlight differences in the perceptions between two samples. These differences suggest that there are different working conditions for the Engineers and the SWOs in their work organizations which affect their perceptions. Thus, their experiences which the respondents brought to the training/learning situation affected the learning situation and training modules need to be designed taking into consideration the experiences of the trainee participants.

The Quality of Work Life (QWL) showed by and large strong positive relationship with the Attitude towards Training variables in case of Engineers, while for the SWOs the correlations were significant, as shown in Table 22, except in one isolated case (i.e., correlation of 'development opportunities' factor of QWL with 'personal growth and development' variable of the ATT). The correlations for the Engineers were significant both at .01 and .05 level of significance whereas for the SWOs the strong correlation emerged at .01 level of significance among all aspects of QWL and the ATT. It may, therefore, be concluded that perception of training was directly and strongly linked with the Quality of Work Life and it was perceived that the training would facilitate improvement in QWL. Contradiction appears between the perceptions in respect of Job Satisfaction and QWL, especially for the SWOs. The working conditions or in other words QWL of the SWOs was although perceived to be improved through training, yet Job Satisfaction was not perceived to be increased by the SWOs, which is indicative of the fact that for the SWOs Job Satisfaction was not as much as was desirable. This state of affairs may be ascribed to the existing working conditions the experiences of which made the SWOs believe that Job Satisfaction could not be brought about through training alone. The conclusions drawn above give rise to the issues of job enrichment requirements, improvement in work environment and effective management, of which training will be a part of the total strategy. The importance of training, therefore, cannot be minimized. The findings in case of the SWOs distinctly point out the importance of training as may be seen from relationship of QWL factors with ATT.

Hypothesis 5: Background Variables will show effect on Attitude towards Training.

The background variables were analysed to study their effect on Attitude towards Training. These variables showed relationship with ATT which are discussed in the following paragraphs:

(i) **Engineers**

(a) **Age:** Table 23 shows that age is significantly but negatively related with only personal growth and development ($r=-.26$, $P<.01$) which supports the hypothesis.

(b) **Pay Scale** : In case of the Engineers pay scale showed comparatively high negative correlation with only personal growth and development ($r=-.36$, $P<.01$), which supports the hypothesis.

(c) **No. of Workers Supervised** : The number of workers supervised directly was subjected to analysis and the variable also had negative relationship with personal growth and development ($r=-.17$, $P<.05$) and with competence the correlation was negative ($r=-.20$, $P<.05$). Thus, findings supported the hypothesis.

(d) **Educational Level** : Contrary to expectations, educational level had significant positive correlations with training effectiveness ($r=.20$. $P<.01$).

(e) **Experience** : Experience had negative correlation with only personal growth and development ($r=-.28$, $P<.01$) which supported the hypothesis.

TABLE 23

Correlation of Background Variables with Attitude Towards Training

Variables	*Background Variables*				
	Age	*Scale of pay*	*No. of workers Supervised directly*	*Educat itonal leave*	*Exper-ience*
Attitude Towards Training					
(a) Training Effectiveness	.06	-.10	-.08	.26*	.05
(b) Personal Growth and Development	-.26*	.36	-.17*	.01	-.28*
(c) Competence	-.01	-.04	-.20**	.05	.02
(d) Gains from Training	.06	-.14	-.14	.05	-.03
(e) Motivation for Personal Growth	.08	-.10	-.04	-.06	-.07

N=130 (ENGINEERS) *$P < .01$ **$P < .05$

(ii) **SWOs:** Table 23 shows the following findings:

(a) **Age** : Age had no relationship with ATT variables.

(b) **Sex:** Sex had no relationship with ATT.

(c) **Pay Scale** : Pay Scale variable showed mixed results, i.e., it was positively related to competence (r=.20, $P < .01$), and negative relationships had been found with the other two variables of ATT, i.e. (a) and (c) (r=.20, $P < .05$) in both the cases.

(d) **No. of Workers Supervised Directly** : In respect of workers supervised Table 23 shows that the Number of Workers Supervised had no relationship with ATT for the SWOs sample. No support to the hypothesis was offered by the variable.

TABLE 24

Correlation of Background Variables with Attitude Towards Training

Variables	*Background Variables*					
	Age	*Sex*	*Pay Scales*	*No. of workers super-vised directly*	*Educa-tional level*	*Expe-rience*
Attitude Towards Training						
(a) Training Effectiveness Personal Growth and Development Motivation for Personal Growth	-.00	.13	-.20	.00	-.20**	-.02
(b) Competence	.11	.02	.20*	.03	-.37*	.15
(c) Personal Growth and Development	.11	.13	-.20*	-.05	-.32*	.04

N=170 (SWOs)

*$P < .01$

**$P < .05$

(e) **Educational Level** : Educational Level showed high negative correlation with variables of ATT and supported the hypothesis.

(f) **Experience** : Experience had no significant correlation with ATT.

The above findings suggest that except the educational level for the Engineers sample and pay scale for SWOs sample which have positive relationship with variables of ATT (one in each case) the background variables do not show any effect on ATT. Thus, the hypothesis is by and large retained and only partially it is not retained.

Hypothesis 6: Training Experience can be predicted by Occupational Aspiration, Job Involvement, Quality of

Work Life, Job Satisfaction, Motivating Potential, and Achievement Value.

The predicting power of the six variables under study, viz.,Occupational Aspiration, Job Involvement, Quality of Work Life, Job Satisfaction, Motivating Potential, and Achievement Value was to be studied and the regression analysis method was used. The correlation values, to some extent, are also indicative of the predictive power of the six independent variables.

(i) **Engineers** : The results of regression analysis of ATT on the six variables are given in the Tables 24-28 for the Engineers. The following part deals with the discussion on regression analysis for both the samples separately.

(a) Regression Analysis of Training Effectiveness

As shown in Table 24 the regression analysis confirms the hypothesis in respect to training effectiveness (F=5.25, $P < .01$).

Individually treated, Job Involvement (F=9.84, $P < .01$), Development Opportunities (QWL) (F=7.67, $P < .01$) Insincerity (QWL) (F=5.58, $P < .01$),Motivating Potential (F=3.35, $P < .05$), and Job Satisfaction (F=5.5, $P < .01$) predicted the training effectiveness.

(b) Personal Growth and Development

The hypothesis is supported by regression analysis (F=6.86, *P* .01). Individually Occupational Aspiration (F=3.32, $P < .05$), Job Involvement (F=18.39, $P < .01$), Motivating Work Climate (QWL) (F=5.27, $P < .01$), Insincerity (QWL) (F=6.83, $P < .05$), Motivating Environment (QWL) (F=7.19, $P < .01$), and Work Values (QWL) (F=4.49, $P < .01$) also supported the hypothesis (Table 25).

The findings of regression analysis clearly show and confirm that these six variables, i.e., Occupational Aspiration, Job Involvement, Quality of Work Life, Job Satisfaction, Motivating Potential and Achievement Value predict the personal growth and development, which is a variable of the Attitude towards Training (obtained through factor loading).

(c) Competence

The regression analysis results are shown in Table 26 which shows that the hypothesis is not supported so far as competence is concerned. (F Value of all the predictor variables is obtained 2.91 which is not significant). However, separately Insincerity, Motivating Environment, Demotivating Climate, and Job Satisfaction are predictive of competence.

The finding leads to the inference that competence cannot be predictied by the six predictor variables.

TABLE 25

Regression Analysis of Training Effectiveness and Occupational Aspiration, Job Involvement, Quality of Work Life, Job Satisfaction, Motivating Potential and Achievement Value.

SL. NO. *VARIABLES*	*B*	*BETA*	*SE OF B*	*F*
1. OCCUPATIONAL ASPIRATION	-.003	-.018	.013	.05
2. JOB INVOLVEMENT	.123	.255	.039	9.84*
3. QUALITY OF WORK LIFE				
(a) Organizational Image	.093	.094	.103	.81
(b) Development Opportunities	.302	.310	.109	7.67*
(c) Organizational Work Style	-.124	-.055	.190	.43
(d) Motivating Work Climate	-.024	-.034	.086	.08
(e) Insincerity	.406	.175	.172	5.58*
(f) Organisational Strategies	.160	.064	.181	.78
(g) Motivating Environment	.234	.103	.207	1.28
(h) Work Values	-.120	-.054	.216	.31
(i) Demotivating Climate	.114	.031	.297	.15
4. MOTIVATING POTENTIAL	-.020	-.137	.011	3.35**
5. JOB SATISFACTION	.043	.192	.018	5.50*
6. ACHIEVEMENT VALUE	.070	.121	.047	2.18

N=130(ENGINEERS)*P<.01**<.05**F=5.25

TABLE 26

Regression Analysis of Personal Growth and Development and Occupational Aspiration, Job Involvement, Quality of Work Life, Job Satisfaction, Motivating Potential and Achievement Value.

SL. NO.	*VARIABLES*	*B*	*BETA*	*SE OF B*	*F*
1.	OCCUPATIONAL ASPIRATION	.019	.131	.010	3.32**
2.	JOB INVOLVEMENT	.130	.323	.030	18.39*
3.	QUALITY OF WORK LIFE				
(a)	Organizational Image	.030	.036	.079	.14
(b)	Development Opportunities	.022	.027	.083	.07
(c)	Organizational Work Style	.099	.052	.145	.46
(d)	Motivating Work Climate	.151	.256	.066	5.27*
(e)	Insincerity	.344	.179	.132	6.83*
(f)	Organizational Strategies	.142	.069	.139	1.04
(g)	Motivating Environment	.425	.225	.158	7.19*
(h)	Work Values	-.350	-.190	.165	4.49**
(i)	Demotivating Climate	.384	.127	.228	2.84
4.	MOTIVATING POTENTIAL	-.004	-.030	.008	.19
5.	JOB SATISFACTION	.010	.052	.014	.48
6.	ACHIEVEMENT VALUE	.32	.067	.036	.77

N=130(ENGINEERS)

*P<.01

**P<.05

F=6.86*

TABLE 27

Regression Analysis of Competence and Occupational Aspiration, Job Involvement, Quality of Work Life, Job Satisfaction, Motivating Potential, and Achievement Value.

SL. NO.	*VARIABLES*	*B*	*BETA*	*SE OF B*	*F*
1.	OCCUPATIONAL ASPIRATION	.017	.139	.011	2.40
2.	JOB INVOLVEMENT	.053	.155	.032	2.75
3.	QUALITY OF WORK LIFE				
	(a) Organizational Image	.009	.014	.083	.01
	(b) Development Opportunities	-.056	-.081	.088	.40
	(c) Organizational Work Style	-.147	-.092	.153	.93
	(d) Motivating Work Climate	.101	.203	.069	2.13
	(e) Insincerity	.374	.230	.139	7.29*
	(f) Organizational Strategies	-.034	-.020	.146	.05
	(g) Motivating Environment	.437	.273	.167	6.87*
	(h) Work Values	-.062	-.040	.174	.13
	(i) Demotivating Climate	.694	.272	.240	8.38*
4.	MOTIVATING POTENTIAL	-.001	-.009	.009	.01
5.	JOB SATISFACTION	.027	.173	.015	3.39
6.	ACHIEVEMENT VALUE	.013	.033	.038	.12

N= 130 (ENGINEERS)

*$P < .01$

**$P < .05$

F=2.91

TABLE 28

Regression Analysis of Gains from Training and Occupational Aspiration, Job Involvement, Quality of Work Life, Job Satisfaction, Motivating Potential and Achievement Value.

SL. NO.	*VARIABLES*	*B*	*BETA*	*SE OF B*	*F*
1.	OCCUPATIONAL ASPIRATION	.009	.096	.008	1.20
2.	JOB INVOLVEMENT	.074	.286	.024	9.66*
3.	QUALITY OF WORK LIFE				
	(a) Organizational Image	-.034	-.064	.063	.30
	(b) Development Opportunities	.012	-.023	.066	.03
	(c) Organizational Work Style	.147	.120	.115	1.62
	(d) Motivating Work Climate	-.012	-.031	.052	.05
	(e) Insincerity	.032	.026	.104	.09
	(f) Organization Strategies	.142	.106	1.110	1.67
	(g) Motivating Environment	.286	.233	.126	5.16*
	(h) Work Values	.125	.105	.131	.91
	(i) Demotivating Climate	.274	.140	.181	2.29
4.	MOTIVATING POTENTIAL	.000	.002	.007	.00
5.	JOB SATISFACTION	.016	.133	.011	2.08
6.	ACHIEVEMENT VALUE	-.003	-.011	0.29	.01

N=130 (ENGINEERS)

*$P < .01$

**$P < .05$

**F=3.15

TABLE 29

Regression Analysis of Motivation for Personal Growth and Occupational Aspiration, Job Involvement, Quality of Work Life, Job Satisfaction, Motivating Potential and Achievement Value.

SL. NO.	*VARIABLES*	*B*	*BETA*	*SE OF B*	*F*
1.	OCCUPATIONAL ASPIRATION	.017	.204	.008	5.18*
2.	JOB INVOLVEMENT	.041	.174	.022	3.43**
3.	QUALITY OF WORK LIFE				
	(a) Organizational Image	-.122	-.249	.059	4.30*
	(b) Development Opportunities	.015	.031	.062	.06
	(c) Organizational Work Style	-.128	-.114	.108	1.42
	(d) Motivating Work Climate	-.014	-.040	.049	.08
	(e) Insincerity	.130	.113	.098	1.77
	(f) Organizational Strategies	.139	.113	.103	1.82
	(g) Motivating Environment	.468	.415	.118	15.83*
	(h) Work Value	.017	.015	.123	.02
	(i) Demotivating Climate	-.272	-.151	.169	2.58
4.	MOTIVATING POTENTIAL	-.016	-.227	.006	6.94*
5.	JOB SATISFACTION	.030	.271	.010	8.27*
6.	ACHIEVEMENT VALUE	.002	.008	.027	.01

N= 130 (ENGINEERS)

*$P < .01$

**$P < .05$

**F=2.89

(d) **Gains from Training**

Table 27 shows that the regression analysis supports the hypothesis (F= 3.15, *P* < 05). Considered alone Job Involvement and motivating environment (QWL) predict gains from training.

(e) **Motivation for Personal Growth**

Motivation for Personal Growth, as the regression analysis in Table 28 shows, is not predicted by the six variables.

The finding does not support the hypothesis although Occupational Aspiration (F=5.18, *P* < .01), Organizational Image (QWL) (F=4.30, *P* < .05), Motivating Environment (QWL) (F=15.83, *P* < .01), Motivating Potential (F=6.94, *P* < .01), and Achievement Value (F=8.27, *P* < .01) are predictive variables for "motivation for personal growth".

On the basis of the above mentioned findings it may be inferred that personal growth and development, gains from training are predicted by the six predictor variables so far as the sample of Engineers is concerned.

(ii) **SWOs**: Regression analysis for SWOs of the "Training effectiveness, personal growth and development, motivation for personal growth" is predicted by the six predictor variables, as shown in Table 29 (F=5.26, *P* < .01). It is evident from Table 29 that Occupational Aspiration, "development opportunities" (QWL). "Organizational image and fairness", and Motivating Potential individually have predictive power to predict" training effectiveness, personal growth and development, motivation for personal growth" as supported by regression analysis (F=3.27, *P* < .05; F=5.73, *P* < .01, and F=8.47, *P* < .01, respectively.

TABLE 30

Regression Analysis of Training Effectiveness, Personal Growth and Development, Motivation for Personal Growth and Occupational Aspiration, Job Involvement, Quality of Work Life, Job Satisfaction, Motivating Potential, and Achievement Value.

SL. NO.	*VARIABLES*	*B*	*BETA*	*SE OF B*	*F*
1.	OCCUPATIONAL ASPIRATION	.070	.167	.039	3.27*
2.	JOB INVOLVEMENT	.007	.010	.058	.01
3.	QUALITY OF WORK LIFE				
	(a) Motivating Work Climate	.016	.018	.070	.06
	(b) Development Opportunities	.196	.200	.082	5.73*
	(c) Organizational Image and Strategies	-.071	-.069	.085	.69
	(d) Organizational Image and Fairness	.220	.194	.091	5.79*
	(e) Work Values	.089	.057	.120	.55
	(f) Insincerity	-.550	-.078	.558	.96
	(g) Organizational Strategies	.174	.035	.450	.15
4.	MOTIVATING POTENTIAL	-.082	-.289	.028	8.47*
5.	JOB SATISFACTION	-.003	-.007	.042	.01
6.	ACHIEVEMENT VALUE	.038	.012	.232	.03

N=170(SWOs)

**P* ,.01

***P* < .05

**F 5.26

TABLE 31

Regression Analysis of Competence and Occupational Aspiration, Job Involvement, Quality of Work Life, Job Satisfaction, Motivating Potential and Achievement Value.

SL. NO.	*VARIABLES*	*B*	*BETA*	*SE OF B*	*F*
1.	OCCUPATIONAL ASPIRATION	.024	.146	.016	2.24
2.	JOB INVOLVEMENT	.024	.088	.024	1.03
3.	QUALITY OF WORK LIFE				
	(a) Motivating Work Climate	.019	.056	.028	.50
	(b) Development Opportunities	-.001	-.003	.034	.00
	(c) Organizational Image and Strategies	.046	.114	.036	1.69
	(d) Organizational Image and Fairness	-.027	-.060	.038	.50
	(e) Work Values	.111	.179	.050	4.92*
	(f) Insincerity	.019	.007	.233	.01
	(g) Organizational Strategies	-.029	-.015	.188	.02
4.	MOTIVATING POTENTIAL	-.003	-.025	.012	.06
5.	JOB SATISFACTION	-.023	-.120	.018	1.77
6.	ACHIEVEMENT VALUE	.030	.023	.097	.10

N=170(SWOs)

$^{*}P < .01$

$^{**}P < .05$

** F=4.09

TABLE 32

Regression Analysis of Personal Growth and Development and Occupational Aspiration, Job Involvement, Quality of Work Life, Job Satisfaction, Motivating Potential, and Achievement Value.

SL. NO.	VARIABLES	B	BETA	SE OF B	F
1.	OCCUPATIONAL ASPIRATION	.005	.120	.004	1.94
2.	JOB INVOLVEMENT	.004	.055	.005	.51
3.	QUALITY OF WORK LIFE				
	(a) Motivating Work Climate	-.002	-.020	.006	.08
	(b) Development Opportunities	.018	.175	.008	5.06*
	(c) Organizational Image and Strategies	.003	.033	.008	.18
	(d) Organizational Image and Fairness	.013	.117	.009	2.41
	(e) Work Values	.020	.123	.011	2.97
	(f) Insincerity	.164	.225	.053	9.49*
	(g) Organizational Strategies	.081	.158	.043	3.56**
4.	MOTIVATING POTENTIAL	-.001	-.047	.003	.26
5.	JOB SATISFACTION	.007	.144	.004	3.25**
6.	ACHIEVEMENT VALUE	.030	.090	.022	1.85

N=170(SWOs)

$*P < .01$

$**P < .05$

**F = 7.08

As shown in Table 30, regression analysis confirms that "competence" can be predicted by Occupational Aspiration, Job Involvement, Quality of Work Life, Job satisfaction, Motivating Potential, and Achievement value ($F=4.09$, $P < .05$). Considering the variables individually, regression analysis in Table 30 reflects that only "Work Value" (QWL) is predictive of "competence" ($F=4.92$, $P < .01$).

Table 31 presents regression analysis and confirms that "personal growth and development" can be predicted by Occupational Aspiration, Job involvement, Quality of Work Life, Job Satisfaction, Motivating Potential, and Achievement Value ($F=7.08$, $P < .01$) whereas singly treated development opportunities (QWL) insincerity (QWL), organizational strategies and Job Satisfaction are predictive of "personal growth and development". ($F=5.06$, $P < .01$, $F=9.49$, $P < .01$, $F=3.56$, $P < .05$, and $F=3.25$, $P < .05$) respectively.

The total regression analysis of Attitude towards Training factors with the six predictor variables in case of Engineers sample lead to the findings that three factors (e.g., Training effectiveness, personal growth and development, gains from training) are predicted by these predictor variables which supports the hypothesis related to predictive power of the six variables in the prediction of Attitude towards training (ATT) (as may be seen in Tables 24, 25, 26, 27 and 28).

TABLE 33

Correlation of Occupational Aspiration, Job Involvement, Quality of Work Life, Motivating Potential, and Achievement Value with Attitude Towards Training.

Variables	*Occupational Aspiration*	*Job involvement*	*Quality of Work Life*** 1	2	3	4	5	6	7	8	9	*Job satisfaction*	*Motivating Potential*	*Achievement Value*
Attitude towards Training														
(a) Training Effectiveness	.09	.41*	.38*	.47*	.16*	.34*	.19*	.14	.21*	.28*	-.07	.38*	.17*	.16*
(b) Personal Growth and Development	.31*	.52*	.28*	.23*	-.03	.36*	.13	.08	.14	.13	.09	.22*	.16*	.16*
(c) Competence	.24*	.37*	.19*	.20*	.07	.33*	.13	-.01	.27*	.23*	.13	.32*	-.01	.19*
(d) Gains from Training	.23*	.38*	.20*	.25*	.17*	.30*	.01	.13	.28*	.32*	.08	.31*	.01	.16*
(e) Motivation for Personal Growth	.28*	.27*	.11	.22*	.01	.23*	.11	-.09	.32*	.22*	-.14	.28*	-.14	.09

N=130 (ENGINEERS)**P*<.01

1. Organizational Image; 2. Development Opportunities; 3. Organisational Work Style; 4. Motivating Work Climate; 5. Insincerity; 6. Organizational Strategies; 7. Motivating Environment; 8. Work Values; 9. Demotivating Climate.

TABLE 34

Correlation of Occupational Aspiration, Job Involvement, Quality of Work Life, Motivating Potential, Achievement Value with Attitude towards Training

Variables	*Occupational Aspiration*	*Job Involvement*	*Quality of Work Life* 1.	2.	3.	4.	5.	6.	7.	*Job satisfaction*	*Motivating Potential*	*Achievement Value*
Attitude towards Training												
(a) Training Effectiveness Personal Growth and Development	.46*	.37*	.25*	.50*	.30*	.50*	.33*	.31*	.42*	-.27*	-.54*	.01
(b) Competence	.37*	.40*	.30*	.23*	.43*	.16*	.42*	.21*	.21*	.35	-.33*	-.01
(c) Personal Growth and Development	.28*	.26*	.26*	.11	.40*	.26*	.35*	.32*	.50*	-.04	-.44*	.16**

N=170 (SWOs) *$P < .01$ **$P < .05$

Quality of Work Life

1. Motivating Work Climate
2. Development Opportunities
3. Organizational Image and Fairness
4. Organizational Image and Strategies
5. Work Values
6. Insincerity
7. Organizational Strategies.

So far as the Social Welfare Officers (SWOs) are concerned (Tables 29,30 and 31 show the results of regression analysis) it may be observed that the three factors of Attitude towards Training are predicted by the six predictor variables under study. The results of regression analysis for SWOs confirm the hypothesis that Attitude towards Training can be predicted by Occupational Aspiration, Job Involvement, Quality of Work Life (QWL), Job Satisfaction, Motivating Potential, and Achievement Value.

Results of the regression analysis for Engineer's sample (which are contained in Tables 24,25,26,27 and 28) partially confirm the hypothesis that the ATT can be predicted by the six predictor variables. In respect of "Competence" and "Motivation for Personal Growth" factors of the ATT the hypothesis is rejected since total variable does not account for the predictive power of these variables, although individually factors of QWL and some predictor variables, such as Job Satisfaction and Job Involvement, predict the "competence" and "Motivation for Personal Growth" factors of ATT.

Correlation of Attitude towards Training with six predictor variables is shown in Table 32 for Engineers and Table 33 for SWOs. Both the samples generally show high positive correlation of ATT with the six predictor variables.

The factor analysis of the Attitude towards Training questionnaire reveals that the Engineer's sample (Table 3 and 4) five factors emerged viz., (1) training effectiveness, (2) personal growth and development, (3) competence, (4) gains from training, and (5) motivation for personal growth and development (Table 31). Similarly for the SWO's sample three factors emerged from factor analysis of ATT e.g., (1) training effectiveness, personal growth and development, motivation for personal growth, (2) Competence, and (3) Personal growth and development as may be seen in Tables 5 and 6. The factor loadings for Engineer's and SWO's sample have been given in Tables 9 and 10 in chapter 6 dealing with development of scale for measuring training experience.

The results of the present study show a positive relationship between Occupational Aspiration and Training Experience and generally a negative relationship in case of Motivating Potential and Training Experience (Measured via Attitude towards Training) in both the samples. Job Satisfaction (i.e., Training Experience) in case of SWOs. The samples, however, show different trends in some other factors like positive relationship between criterion variable and Job Satisfaction in case of Engineers and the negative relationship between the two variables. Results are indicative of different training experience in two organizations.

Further evidence of differences in the samples of two organizations is reflected by mean values shown in Table 34 for Engineers and Table 35 for the SWOs sample. Figures followed by the Tables 33 and 34 showing differences in mean values of the Training Experience questionnaire variables also clearly point out different profiles in two organizations.

TABLE 35

Variable	*Mean*
Training Experience	
(Attitude Towards Training)	
(a) Training Effectiveness	16.78
(b) Personal Growth and Development	15.35
(c) Competence	15.18
(d) Gains from Training	11.75
(e) Motivation for Personal Growth	7.10

N=130 (ENGINEERS)

TABLE 36

Variable	*Mean*
Training Experience	
(Attitude Towards Training)	
(a) Training Effectiveness. Personal Growth and Development, Motivation for Personal Growth	35.67
(b) Competence	16.49
(c) Personal Growth and Development	4.08

N= 170 (SWOs)

Comparison of mean values of the factors of Attitude towards Training for the two samples is shown in Figures 6, 7, 8, 9., 10 and 11.

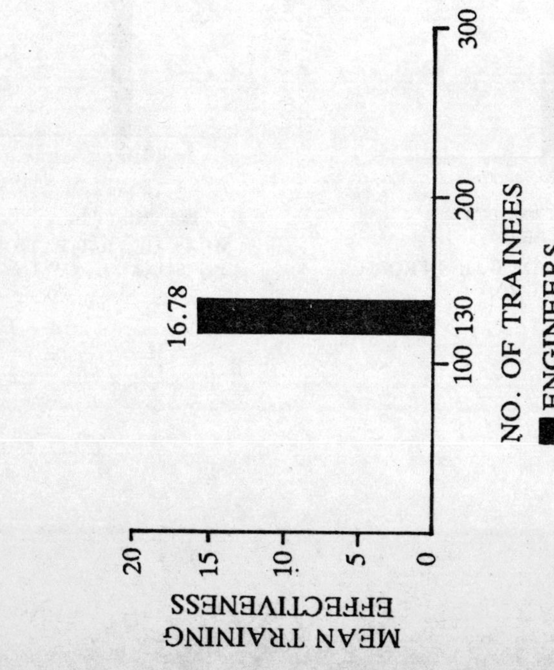

Figure. 6. **MEAN OF TRAINING EFFECTIVENESS**

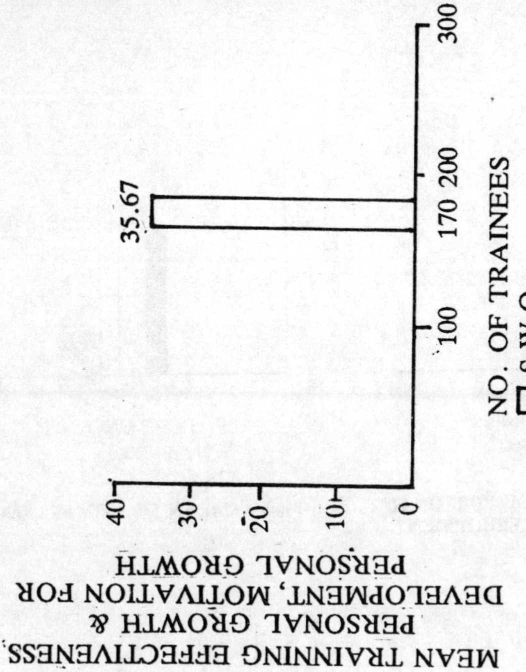

Figure 7. **MEAN OF TRAINNING EFFECTIVENESS, PERSONAL GROWTH & DEVELOPMENT, MOTIVATION FOR PERSONAL GROWTH**

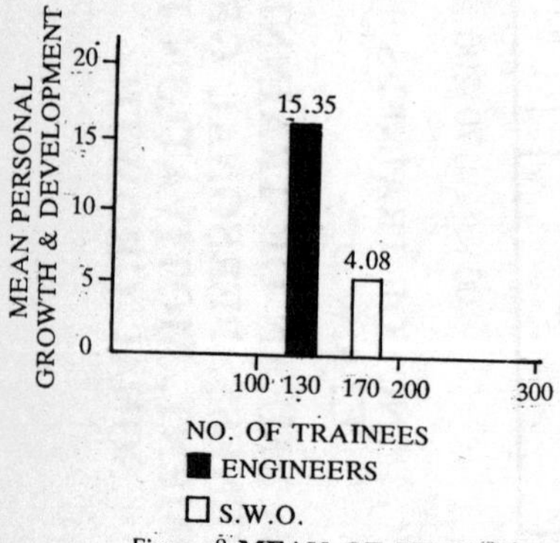

Figure 8. **MEAN OF PERSONAL GROWTH & DEVELOPMENT**

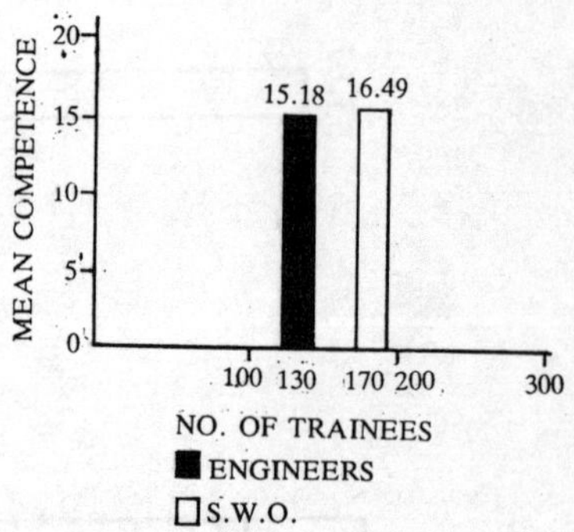

Figure 9. **MEAN OF COMPETENCE**

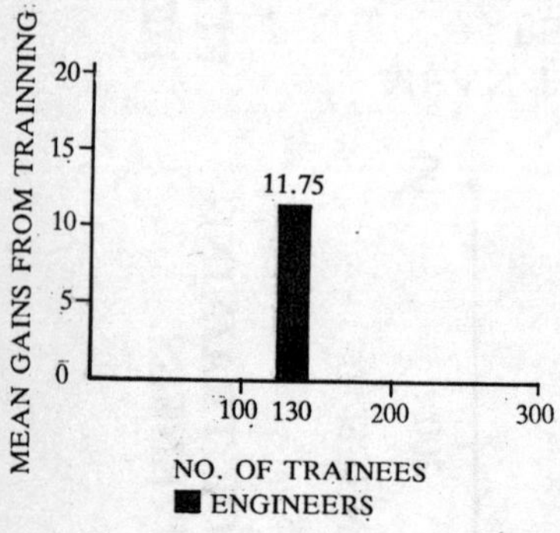

Figure 10. **MEAN OF GAINS FROM TRAINING**

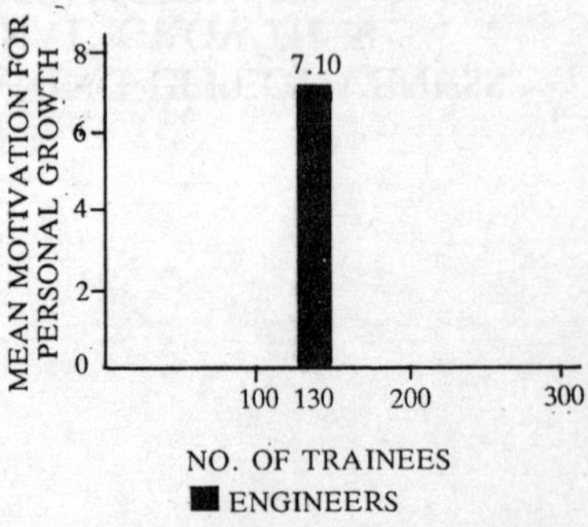

Figure 11. **MEAN OF MOTIVATION FOR PERSONAL GROWTH**

Tables 33 and 34 show the mean values of Attitude Training. Table 33 shows that average for Engineers' sample with respect to Training Effectiveness is 16.78 and corresponding factor of "training effectiveness, personal growth and development, motivation for personal growth" in case of SWOs, as shown by Table 34, has a mean value of 35.67.

Thus, on the basis of mean values, it is clear that the two samples show a difference of 18.89 in means.

Engineers sample shows that competence has an average value of 15.18 as against an average value of 16.49 in case of SWOs with a difference of 1.31 in the average of both the samples.

Gains from training, as shown by Table 33, has a mean value of 11.75 for Engineers' sample whereas SWO's sample has no corresponding factors.

Motivation for personal growth in case of Engineers has a mean value of 7.10. Factor analysis revealed that in SWO's sample motivation for personal growth factor combined with training effectiveness and personal growth and development factors and did not emerge as a separate factor of Attitude towards Training.

Personal growth and development has a mean value of 15.35 for Engineers' sample and 4.08 in case of SWOs. There is difference of 11.27 in the two main values.

On the basis of correlational analysis and mean values it can be concluded that the two organizations have distinctly different profiles in respect of psychological correlates. The findings of regression analysis further support that the two organizations have different profiles. The study has established that psychological correlates do have influence on training experience which is predictable by the psychological correlates under the present investigation. Parmeswaran (1983), Clark (1975), Anderson (1986), Brinkerhoff (1986) have also emphasized on the importance of psychological correlates and the psychological bases to behaviour. The conceptualizations based on individual differences and the psychological correlates to behaviour have been proven to have definitive role in the training situation and the training experiences. The results find support especially from the conceptualizations by Parmeswaran (1983). The findings of the present investigation are indicative of the fact that psychological factors are important in determining training experiences which are specifically based on perception of individual trainees.

The hypothesis that training experience can be predicted by Occupational Aspiration, Job Involvement, Quality of Work Life, Job Satisfaction, Motivating Potential and Achievement Value strongly suggests that design of training programmes and training strategies must take into account these psychological correlates of MD training. Further, the psychological factors affecting the individual trainee and the motivational possibilities that are brought by him to the training situation must be taken into account and design of a training programme and its contents will be largely determined on the psychological factors and motivational possibilities affecting individual trainees. As discussed earlier, the importance of psychological factors and individual differences need to be considered to design meaningful training programmes, however, not much of thought has been given in this direction by the management of organizations, top officials responsible for policy decisions at Governmental level so far as public sector organizations are concerned, especially loss-incurring (non-profit making) 'sick' units/enterprises which gave rise to problems of serious nature. Training is an important strategy to bring about HRD and in optimization of HRD. The developmental effort have not been made to the desired level in other "non-sick" public sector organizations also. Singh and Pant (1983) have reported their findings based on perceptions of the public sector managers who have clearly stated the unfortunate state of affairs in the public sector organizations. Various interferences, inability of the management to function effectively due to total centralization of powers with the top management and other related problems as reported by Singh and Pant (1983) have resulted in unsatisfactory performance, low productivity as compared to private sector enterprises, and feelings of dissatisfaction among managers from the organizational environment, policies and decisions of autocratic type fully influenced by the bureaucratic functioning. These situations are as such demotivating and there is no scope for personal growth and development for managers. In addition little or no concern for developmental efforts have created non-conducive work environment which gives rise to low productivity, demotivated employees and managers, losses, heavy investments by the Government in sick public sector organizations getting no returns in terms of profits / productivity and there is overall unsatisfactory performance. Wherever training is organized by in the trainers and the management merely as a routine exercise and just a formality with no concern for making training programmes effective and useful for trainee managers. The manager also shows a lukewarm interest or treat the training as a routine exercise; since they unwillingly attend training without active involvement as trainees. In this context the review by Raghavachari (1983) is pertinent according to which the management training process during the past quarter of a century was in an unhappy position. The efficacy of training in public sector organizations, therefore, demands serious concern.

Feedback from those being trained from time to time, if not on regular basis, is of crucial importance, which has practically been experienced by the author being a training course director and trainer himself. A continuous in-flow system of feedback in close liason and coordination with the personnel departments of trainee managers' organization(s) should be developed so that continuous feedback is ensured on one hand, and on the other personal visits of trainers to their organizations after their training should be made a permanent feature for the formulation of training strategies and improvements in the contents of training programmes. These visits would facilitate the trainers and in training module planning the inclusions of topics pertaining day-to-day problems and bottlenecks being experienced by the managers in real life situation (i.e. on their job).

Individual differences have been experienced to have overwhelming influence than the background variables. However, the effect of background variables cannot totally be negated. The organizational quality of work life, organizational strategies, and actual working conditions affect the attitude of trainees towards training. If training is a necessary requirement and trainees are not motivated for training their receptivity is adversely affected besides other effects and their attitude towards training has been found to be negative and they unwillingly enter into training situation leading to ineffective training, whereas there are no lacunae in the training efforts, training contents and efficacy of training, thus, is worst suffered. It has also been observed that during a training programme when capsule/subparts/components-wise training is imparted to enable the participants better understanding of basic concepts and ideas, learn requisite skills, and other such items as may be made part of the training syllabus/module a subpart or component or capsule-wise evaluation by trainees as well as an overall evaluation of the training programme on completion of a programme proved useful for getting valuable feedback. The overall experiences, in evaluation offer an opportunity to trainees, on one hand to express frank and free reactions/responses about their evaluation of the training and on the other, provide a scope for further improvement in future training programmes.

A feedback from their employers also facilitates trainers to improve the future training. In fact, the feedback process should ideally be a two-way process in which not only trainers obtain a feedback from employers but the employers or senior management should also get a feedback from trainers about the performance of trainees during the training programme. So far as feedback for trainers from trainees on training programme is concerned much depends upon the type of trainees attending training programmes. At this stage also attitude of trainees towards training has an important role in terms of degree to which training has been treated seriously by them and accordingly reactions/responses of participants show considerable amount of variations.

Finally, it may be said that the model proposed for the present study gets strong support by the results. The study is explained well by the model and offers support to the Humanistic-Organismic perspective for designing future MD training programmes. The study further highlights the importance of the Humanistic-Organismic perspective and suggests directions to formulate overall HRD strategies in the organizations in general and public sector organizations in particular. The Humanistic-Organismic approach has been successfully used in achieving the objectives of HRD and OD in the United States and is becoming popular in Europe and West. However, the 'Quality circles' of Japan could not yield desirable results in the U.S. organizations, and were only partially successful elsewhere. Therefore, the better alternative before the managements which also has universal applicability potential, is the Humanistic-Organismic approach and it has led to popularity of personal development training programmes. The personal development training aims at developing the manager as a person first to become an effective manager also. These training programmes have been widely used for personal growth and development of managers in the U.S.A. On the basis of encouraging results and the success stories being reported for optimizing HRD and OD and in terms of increased productivity and better performance of the organizations this approach would provide solutions to a number of nagging problems of serious dimensions in organizations, particularly in the Indian public sector organizations. Today a great degree of emphasis is laid on the HRD and its processes, and in the present context an insight is offered to take a note of human factors and develop processes conducive to better performance as well as the productivity and development of public sector organizations to meet out the challenge of providing healthy and rapid industrial advancements, which was the basic purpose for mixed economy concept.

8

CONCLUSIONS AND RECOMMENDATIONS

This chapter is designed to offer conclusions drawn, based on the results of the investigation and certain recommendations have been reported. The strategies which would facilitate the Management Development training also appear in the form of recommendations.

The following conclusions emerge from this study :

1. The present study substantiates the proposition that attitudes and perceptions of individual affect the training experiences. This is indicative of the fact that individual differences are important in training experience. This also leads to better understanding and importance of job enrichments strategies of organization leading to Organizational Development (OD) and personal growth and development of employees. Motivation, learning, perception and personal growth are important psychological processes that affect the training and work experiences. Results of the study have distinctly shown the key role of personality and perceptual factors in affecting the Training Experiences significantly.

2. Background variables generally do not have influence on the training experiences.

3. In this study comparison of the two organizations clearly suggest that in the design of training programmes the type of participants in training programmes must be given due consideration.

4. The factor analysis reveals specific dimensions of quality of work life and training experience; some of the dimensions differed in the two organizations which may only be attributed to (a) difference in perceptions, (b) work environment, and (c) different areas of job although the basic nature of job was management for the two samples. The response pattern also varied between the two samples which was apparent to the extent that it appeared even in the raw data on various items of different tools being used in the study.

5. The present study was an attempt to identify some psychological correlates of Management Development training programmes and the results have supported that psychological correlates (the six variables under investigation) strongly affected the training experiences.

6. It has strongly been highlighted that job characteristics as identified by Hackman and Lawler (1971) play an important role to provide the job motivating potential which is one of the crucial variable and affects training experiences vitally

Thus, the conclusions provide a strong support to have concern for psychological correlates, including the individual differences forming part of distinctness in personality of managers in no case should be ignored. Rather the psychological correlates should be used to determine the design of training contents and methodology for imparting training. The experience and observations of the author discussed in the final part of the preceding chapter on results and discussion emphatically substantiate the findings and the conclusions drawn on the basis of results of the study. Hence, importance of psychological correlates needs special concern in the design of MD training modules.

Recommendations

Based on the findings of the present study some recommendations are made, which would facilitate the MD training programme planners, the top management and the concerned officials of the Government, especially for purposes of public sector organisations and government departments. These recommendations may be treated valid also for other organizations. The recommendations are as follows :

1. Management development training programmes should take into account the personality factors and individual differences. Appropriate and relevant learning theories should be applied for meaningful and enriching training experiences.

2. Management development training is closely related to human resource development (HRD). The trainer's role in the training process is of utmost importance. A trainer is perceived as a learning specialist, an administrator, a training director, an information coordinator, and a consultant to management. A trainer is, thus, a leader and as a leader, a trainer or a training director provides direction and persuades managers to a newer approach to look at everything. Thus, attempts are made through the training process to inculcate right type of perceptions and attitudes which are required to effectively discharge duties assigned and to fulfill the expectations as specified in the job responsibilities/job chart. This is necessary in addition to development of necessary skills required for successful and effective functioning in accordance with the job responsibilities. These basics are applicable to every type of training and every area of varied job tasks for different jobs having different nature of job tasks. The investigation also recommends designing and development of training programmes taking into consideration the needs of individual manager trainee in order to cater to their real training needs that must be given due and proper concern. Therefore it would be a fruitful exercise to do needs analysis which would consider job skills related to the job and personal needs for growth and development to be an effective manager and a wholesome person to become the 'manager' in the truest sense of the word. Based on the findings of

the present study training strategies and content may be revised and more appropriate training programmes in public sector organizations may be designed, which could take into account the crucially important fact of individual differences among trainees in order to increase the need based efficacy of training for managers and management development. Personal growth and development is equally important as is the professional growth and development. This fact should be given due weightage in designing training modules.

3. In case of public sector organizations as well as other organizations, where training has still not been recognized and used as a crucially important strategy and method for manager and management development to bring about HRD, OD and MD training should essentially be made an organizational policy and the training process should be introduced so as to tackle the problem of sick public sector enterprises/units.

4. If training organizers take a note of suggested strategies and job enrichment is introduced the motivated managers would take training and better cost-effective results could be achieved. The real solution in enriching the jobs, as has been mentioned above, training is frequently been viewed as a job enrichment strategy. Encouraging results may be achieved through snowball effect which would begin by introduction of training where training has not been given importance and in the organizations/government departments where HRD efforts are already initiated through training, improvement in the training programmes based on feedbacks, psychological factors affecting training experience, and individual differences among trainees are attempted.

9

LIMITATIONS OF THE STUDY AND SUGGESTIONS FOR FUTURE RESEARCH

This chapter acknowledges the limitations of the present study and offers suggestions for further research in the area. As may be seen from the review of related literature there was a gap that no attention was paid to the importance and role of psychological factors and individual differences in the training situation and training experiences. The investigation, therefore, was an attempt to fill this gap in research. This piece of research on one hand fulfils the need for research and on the other suggests some of the practical steps which would facilitate the trainers and would enhance, it is hoped at least to some extent, the efficacy of training. The study was undertaken with an ambitious planning but due to a number of practical constraints and to keep a time frame in order to reach meaningful and practically useful findings, there are some limitations of the study which have been mentioned below :

1. The present study was conducted in two government sector training organizations. Study in private sector training organizations may be conducted to explore differences, if, any, in

the private-sector training organizations imparting management development training to managers.

2. Seven psychological correlates have been studied in the present research. Future researches may be designed to study the effects of additional factors such as orientation, work value, group atmosphere, and intrinsic, motivation may have bearing on training experiences.

3. Future exploration on the effects of job/task characteristics dimensions might add to knowledge in this area of research.

4. In view of the findings of the present study, job enrichment exercises may be planned as action research projects in different organizations.

5. Training organizations may take up longitudinal research projects and useful programmes may be planned using the findings of such similar research projects as the present study.

BIBLIOGRAPHY

Adelberg, M.1969 : Industrial training of the hard core unemployed. Personnel. Psychol., 46, 6,22-27.

Agarwal, M.C.,1983 : Management training problems in the public sector. In R.K. Mishra and S. Ravishankar : Management Development and Training in Public Enterprises. Ajanta Publications, New Delhi, 183-196.

Aldag, R.J., and Brief : A.P., 1979 : Task design and employee motivation, Gelenview, IL:Scott, Foresman.

Amarchand, D., 1983 : Management Development and Training: Its Role in Public Enterprises Development. In R.K. Mishra and S. Ravishankar : Management Development in Public Enterprises, Ajanta Publications, New Delhi, 1-28.

Anderson, E., 1986 : Stroke your folks: Build subordinates' esteem. Training, January 13-14.

Anderson,R.C.,1967 : Individual differences and problems solving. In Learning and Individual Differences, ed., R.M. Gagne, Columbus, Ohio:Merril.

Anderson, R.C., Faust, G.W., Roderick, M.C. 1968 : Overprompting in programme instruction. J. Educ. Psychol., 59,88-93.

Andrews, Kenneth R., 1957 (a): "Is Management Training Effective? I. Evaluation by Managers and Instructors". Harvard Business Review, January-February.

Andrews, Kenneth R., (1957b) :"Is Management Training Effective II. Measurement, Objectives and Policy", Harvard Business Review, March, April.

Anshen, Melvin, 1955 : "Better Use of Executive Development Programs", Harvard Business Review, November-December.

Argyris, Chris, 1956 : "Executive Development Programmes;: Some unresolved problems, "Personnel, July.

Attwood, D.A., and Wiener, E.L., 1969 : Automated instruction for vigilance training. J.Appl. Psychol, 53, 3, 218-23.

Bach, George L., 1951 : "Where Do Executives Come From?" The Executive and Health, Transactions Bulletin No. 19, Industrial Hygiene Foundation, Mellon Institute, Pittsburg

Baker, W.E.,1978 : Certain dimensions of job content and their relationship to job satisfaction, Dissert. Abs. Int., 39,5, Nov., 2551 - B.

Balling, S.S., (1982) : Extensions of neo-Hullian learning theory to selected areas of management. Dissert. Abst. Int., 42,7, January, 3021-B.

Bandura, A., 1969 : Principles of Behaviour Modification. New York : Holt, Rinehart and Winston.

Barlett, A.C., 1967 : Changing behaviour as a means to increased efficiency. J.Appl. Behav. Sci.,3, 381-403.

Bass, B.M., and Vaughan, J.A.,1986 : Training in Industry. The Management of Learning. Belmont, Calif : Wadsworth.

Baumgartel, H. et.al., 1978 : How organizational climate and personality affect the pay-off from advanced management training sessions. Kans. Bus. Rev., 5, 1-10.

Beer, M. 1969 : A Systems Approach to Organizations Development. Presented at American Psychol. Association Meeting, Washington, D.C.

Benedict, B.A., et.al.(1967): The clinical-experimental approach to assessing organizational change efforts. J.Appl. Behav.Sci., 3,3,347-80.

Berglund, G.W.,1969 : The effect of partial reinforcement in programmed instruction. Progr. Learn. Educ. Tech, 6, 102.-8.

Berelson Bernard, and Stenier, Garry, A., 1964 : Human Behaviour - An Inventory of Scientific Findings. Harcourt, Brace, and World.

Berrien, E.E.,1968 : General and Social Systems. New Brunswick, N.J., Rutgers Univ.Press.

Blake, R.R., and Mouton, J.S., 1968 : Corporate Excellence Through Grid Organization Development. Houston : Gulf.

Blake, R-R. and Mouton, J.S. 1970 : OD—Fad of Fundamental. Train. Develo.J.,24,1,9-17.

Blum, M.L., Naylor,J.C.,1968 : Industrial Psychology:Its theoretical and social foundations. New York: Harper and Row.

Blum, M.L. and Naylor,J.C., 1984 : Industrial Psychology, (1st Ed.), CBS Publishers, New Delhi, 251-252.

Blum, M.L. and Naylor J.C., 1984 : Industrial Psychology (1st Ed.) CBS Publishers, New Delhi, p.252.

Boyd. J.B., and Elliss, J.D., 1962 : Findings of Research into Senior Management Seminars. Hydro-Electric Power. Commission of Ontario, Toronto.

Briggs, G.E., and Naylor J.C., 1965 : Team versus individual training, training task fidelity, and task organization effects on transfer performance by three-man teams. J.Appl. Psychol., 49,6,387-92.

Briggs, G.E., and Johnston, W.A., 1966 " Stimulus and response fidelity in team training. J.Appl. Psychol.50,2,114-17.

Brinkerhoff, Robbert O., 1986 : Expanding Needs Analysis. Training and Development Journal. American Society for Training and Development Inc., Alexandria, Va., February, 64-65.

Brinkman, E.H., 1986 : Programmed instruction as a technique for improving spatial visualization. J.Appl. Psychol.,50,2,179-84.

Brousseau, K.R.,1977 : Effects of job experience on personality: A theoretical and emperical investigation Dissert. Abs. Int., 37, 11, May, 5868 B-69-B.

Buchanan, P.C., 1969 : Laboratory training and organization development. Admin. Sci. Quart., 14,466-79.

Beuhler, R.E., (1969) : Job related behaviour, rating scale. Train. Develo.J.,23,3,14-21.

Bunker, D.R., 1965 : Individual application of laboratory training. J.Appl,Behav.Sci.,1, 137-47.

Bunker,D.R., and Knowles, E.S., 1967 : Comparison of behavioural changes resulting from human relations training laboratories of different lengths. J.Appl.Behav.Sci.,3,4,505-24.

Burcin, W.A., 1967 : General Skills training program Train. Develop. J., 21,12,9-11.

Burke, R.J. 1969 : A plea for a systematic evaluation of training Train. Develop. J., 23,8,24-29.

Burris, R., 1968 : Programmed learning. In the international Encyclopaedia of the Social Sciences, 182-88. New York: Macmillan and The Free Press.

Byars, L.L., and Crane, D.P., 1969 : Training by objectives. Train. Develop. J., 23,6,38-49.

Cahoon, D.D., Paterson, L.P., and Watson, C.G., 1968 : Relative effectiveness of programmed text and teaching as a function of measured interests. J.Appl.Psychol.,52,6,454-56.

Campbell, R.D., 1969 : United States military training in cross cultural interaction. Alexandria, Va.:Matrix Corp.

Campbell, J.P.,et.al.,1970 : Managerial Behaviour, Performance and Effectiveness. New York : Mc Graw-Hill.

Campbell.J., 1971 : Personnel training and development. Annual Rev. of Psychol., 22, 565-602.

Carter, A.G., 1983 : QWL; An exploratory study in worker groups. Dissert. Abst. Int., 44,5, Nov., 1626-B.

Cavanagh, P., and Jones, C., 1968 : An evaluation of the contribution of a program of self instruction to management training. Progr. Learn. Educ. Tech.5,294-301.

Chakraborty, S.K., 1983: Training for corporate / planning in Public sector enterprises. In R.K. Mishra and S. Ravishankar(eds): Management Development and Training in Public Enterprises. Ajanta Publications, New Delhi, 225-238.

Chaney, F.B., and Teel, K.S., 1967 : Improving Inspector perfórmance through training and visual aids. J. Appl. Psychol,51,4,311-15.

Choudhary, L.H., 1983 : Training and development in the 1980s and after. In R.K. Mishra and S. Ravishankar : Management Development and Training in Public Enterprises. Ajanta Publication, New Delhi, 197-216.

Chemers, M.M., 1969 : Cross-cultural training as a means for improving situational favourableness. Hum. Relat., 22, 6, 531-46.

Chermick, J., and Smith, G., 1969:Employing the disadvantage. In D.B. Deoringer (ed). : Programs to Employ the disadvantaged. Englewood Cliffs., N;J. : Prentice-Hall.

Childs, J.M., et. al., 1981 : The effects of pilot experience on acquiring instrument flight skills: Phase I, U.S. Dep. Transp. Fed. Aviat. Admn. Washington, D.C.

Clark, P.A., 1975 : Intervention Theory : Matching role, focus, and content. In E.Davis and A.B. Cherns : Quality of working life, Vol.I, 177-192.

Common, C.A., 1969 : The managerial surface. Train. Develop. J., 23, 10, 12-19.

Cook, C.,.1967 : Programmed instruction in selling. Train. Develop J., 21, 7, 34-40.

Connor, D.V., 1968 : Teaching engineering student by machine and text. Progr. Learn. Educ. Tech. 5,129-36.

Cooper, G.L., 1969 : The influence of the trainer on participant change in T-groups. Hum. Relat., 22,6,515-30.

Cornell, P.T., 1985 : Condition influencing job performance and QWL in a data entry task. Dissert. Abst. Int., 46,1, July, 336-B.

Cornbach, L.J., 1967 : How can instruction be adapted to individual differences ? In Gagne, R.M. (ed.) 1967 : Learning and Individual Difference Columbus, Ohio " Merril.

Culbert, S.A., 1968 : Trainer self-disclosure and member growth in two T-groups.J.Appl.Behav.Sci.4,1,47-74.

Dacher, H.P.1969 : The effects of performance feedback on attribution of casuality for performance and satisfaction. Dissertation Abstracts International, 31,2,190,941-B.

Davis, L.E., and Cherns, A.B.(eds), 1975 : The quality of working life : Problems, prospects and the state of Art: Volume one, The Free Press, New York.

De, N.R., 1983 : Do Indian managers play as a team. In R.K. Mishra and S. Ravishankar : Management Development and Training in Public Enterprises, Ajanta Publications, New Delhi, 153-162.

De Bettignies, H.C., 1925 : Management development; The International perspective. In B. Taylor and G.L. Lippitt (eds.), Management Development and Training Handbook, McGraw-Hill Book Co., London, p.4.

Delbecq, A.L., 1970 : Sensitivity training. Train Develop. J. 24, 1, 32-35.

Dholakia, B.H., 1983 : Improving public enterprise performance through management development. In R.K. Mishra and S. Ravishankar (eds.). Management Development and Training in Public Enterprises. Ajanta Publications, New Delhi, 279-288.

Dick. W., and Lotta., R., 1969 : Comparative effects of ability and presentation mode in computer assisted instruction and programme instruction. Tech.memo, computer-assisted Instruc. Cent.,Florida State Univ.

Doeringer, D.B. (ed.), 1969 : Programs to Employ the disadvantage Englewood Cliffs, N.J. :Prentice-Hall.

Doraiswami, P.K.,1983 : Management Development: A conceptual framework. In R.K. Mishra and S. Ravishankar (eds.) : Management Development and Training in Public Enterprises. Ajanta Publications, 2.11.

Dunham, R.B., 1984 : Organizational Behaviour : People and Processes in Management, Richard D. Irwin, Inc., Homewood, Illionois.

Fernandes, P.J. 1983 : Educating managers and managing educators. In R.K.Mishra and S.Ravishankar: Management Development and Training in Public Enterprises. Ajanta Publications, New Delhi : 129-152.

Fernandes, P.J., 1983: Training Public Enterprises Managers:Some questions, issues, and dilemmas. In R.K.Mishra and S.Ravishankar : Management Development and Training in Public Enterprises. Ajanta Publications, New Delhi, 97-112.

Finston, H.V., 1969 : Impact of T-Group training, within an R & D environment. Personnel, J., 4892, 108-14.

Fishbein, M.A.,(ed.) 1967 : Readings in attitude theory and measurement. New York. Wiley.

Flanagan, J.C.,1968 : Individualizing Education. Paper presented at the American Psychological Association Convention. San Francisco.

Fleishman, E.A.,1987 : Individual differences and motor learning. In Learning and Individual Differences, Columbus, Ohio " Merril.

Folley, J.D., Jr., 1969 : Determining training needs of department store sales personnel. train. Develop. J., 23, 7, 24-27.

Foreman, W.J., 1967 : Management Training in Large Corporations. Training and Development Journal, 21,5,11-17.

Foster, R.J.,1969 : Dimensions of training of overseas assignments, George Washington Univ.Hum. Resour. Res. Office.

Frank, H.E., and Smith, P.J., 1969 : A British impression of the American training scene. Train. Develop. J., 23,1,20-23.

French,J.R.P., Sherwood, J.J., and Bradford, D.L,1966 : Changes in self-identity in a management training conference. J.Appl. Behav. Sci., 2, 210-18.

Friedlander, F., 1968 : A comparative study of consulting processes and group development. J. Appl. Behav. Sci., 4,4, 377-400.

Gagne, R.M., 1962 : Military training and principles of learning. American Psychol., 18, 83-91.

Gagne, R.M. et.al., 1962 : Factors in acquiring knowledge of a mathematical task-Psychol. Mongor.76:Whole No.526.

Gagne, R.M. and Briggs L.I., 1974 : Principles of Instructional Design. New York. Holt, Rinehart and Winston.

Ganguly, D.S., 1983 : Management development in public corporations. In R.K. Mishra and S. Ravishankar (eds.). Management Development and Training in Public Enterprises. Ajanta Publications, New Delhi, 403-428.

Gavin,J.F.,1969 : Ability, Efforts and Role Perception as Antecedents of Job Performance. Psychological Abstracts, 30, 8, 1970.

Glimer, B. Von Heller and Deci, Edward L., 1977 : Industrial and Organizational Psychology (4th edn) Mc Graw Hill Book Co. N.Y.

Glaser, R. (ed.), 1962 : Training Research and Education. Pittsburgh, Pa : University of Pittsburg Press.

Glaser, R., 1967 : Some implications of previous work on learning and individual differences. In Gagne, R.M. (ed.)1967 : Learning and Individual differences. Columbus, Ohio : Merill.

Glaser, R. 1982 : Instructional Psychology, Past, Present and Future, Am. Psychol. 37, 292-305.

Glickman, A.S., and Vallence, T.R., 1958 : Curriculum assessment with critical incidents J.Appl. Psychol, 42, 329-35.

Golambiewski, R.T., and Bhumberg, A., 1967 : Training and Relational learning : The confrontation design. Training Develop. J., 21, 11,35-43.

Gomersell, E.R., and Myers, M.S., 1966 : Break through in on the job training. Harvard Bus. Rev., 44, 4, 62-72.

Grady, J.F., Jr. 1985 : An investigation of the relationship between employee participation in quality circles and changes in their work life quality and productivity. Dissert. Abst. Int. 46, 3, Sept., 1989.

Graves, G.P.,1968 : Initial sales training. Train.Develop.J.,22, 8, 26-30.

Griffin, R.W.,1982 : Task design : An integrative approach, Glenview, IL : Scott, Foresman.

Greinsley, D.L., 1969 : Acquisition, retention, and retraining : Effects of high and low fidelity in training devices. George Washington Univ. Hum. Resour. Res. Off.

Hackman, J.R., and Lawler, E.E.,III,1971 : Employee reactions to job characteristics. Journal of Applied Psychology Monograph, 55, 259-286.

Hackman, J.R. and Oldham, G.R., 1975 : Development of the job diagnostic survey. Journal of Applied Psychology, 60, 159-170.

Hagman, J.D.,1980 : Effects of training task repetition on retention and transfer of maintenance skill. Res. Rep. 1271, Alexandria, Va.

Hall,J., and Williams, M.S., 1970 : Group dynamics training and improved decision making, J. Appl. Behav. Sci., 6, 39-68.

Hallestein, R.W., 1969 : We know where to start. Train. Develop. J., 23,7,32-33.

Hammerton M., and Tickner, A.H., 1967 : Visual factors affecting transfer of training from a simulated to a real control situation. J. Appl. Sci., 51, 1, 46-49.

Handa, K.L., 1983 ; Training in performance budgeting. In R.K. Mishra and S. Ravishankar (eds) Management Development and Training in Public Enterprises. Ajanta Publications, New Delhi, 455-470.

Harmon, P., 1968 " A classification of performance objective behaviours in job training programmes. Educ. Technol., 8, 22, 11-16.

Harris, E.F. and Fleishman, E.A., 1955(a) : Human relations in training and the stability of leadership patterns. Journal of Applied Psychology, 39, 20-25.

Harris and Fleishmen 1955(b) *Ibid*. Effects of management development on manager behaviour and subordinate perception, 22, 4, 38-50.

Harris, W.A., and Vincent, N.L., 1967 : Comparison of performance of sales training graduates and non-graduates. J. Appl. Psychol., 51, 5, 436-41.

Harrison, R., and Lubin, B., 1965 : Personal style, group composition, and learning. J. Appl., Behav. Sci., 1, 286-301.

Hartley, J., 1968 : Some factors affecting student performance in programmed learning. Progr. Learn. Educ. Tech. 5,206-18.

Hellervick, L. 1969 : Project 250 : An Evaluation. Minneapolis, Minn.Personnel Decisions.

Herdberg, R. Steffen, H., and Baxter, B., 1965 : Insurance fundamentals-A Programmed text versus a conventional text. Personnel Psychol. 18, 2, 165-72.

Harrison, R., and Hopkins, R.L., 1967 : The design of cross cultural training : An alternative to the university model. J. Appl. Behav. Sci., 3,4, 431-60.

Herman, J.B. and Hulin, C.L., 1972 : Studying organizational Attitudes from individual and organizations frames of reference. Organizational Behaviour and Human Performance, 8, 84-108.

Hersey. P., and Kellner, C.A., 1968 : A behavioural approach to training the sales force. Train. Develop. J., 22, 11, 1-9.

Hersey, P., and Blanchard, K.H., 1969 : Life cycle theory of leadership. Train. Develop. J., 23, 5, 26-35.

Herzberg, F. 1959 : The motivation to work. New York : Wiley.

Hilgard Ernest R., 1956 : Theories of Learning. Appleton-Century-Crofts,p.290.

Hinrichs, J.R., 1971 : Ability correlates in learning a psychomotor task. J. Appl. Psychol., 1971.

Hodgson J.D., and Bremer, M.H., 1968 : Successful experience: Training Hardcore unemployed. Harvard Bus. Rev., 46, 5, 148-56.

Hulin, C.L., and Alvarez, K., 1970 : Changing task structure and changing subjects : A comparison of two explanations of changing correlations. Urbana: Univ. Illinois.

Humphrey, L.G., 1960 : Investigations of the simplex. Psychometrika, 4, 313-23.

House,R.J., 1967 : Management Development : Design, Evaluation and implementation. Ann Arbor : University of Michigan, Bureau Industr. Relat.

Jafee, C.L., and Friar, L., 1969 : Use of simulation in training disadvantaged employees for secretarial positions. Train. Develo. J., 23, 8, 30-37.

Jensen, A.R., 1967 : Varieties of individual differences in learning. In R.M. Gagne (ed) : 1967 : Learning and Individual differences. Columbus, Ohio : Merril.

Johnson, K.A., 1968 : The effect of topic distribution within programmed instructional booklets. U.S. Govt. Res. Rep. 68, 6,30.

Johnston, W.A., 1966 : Transfer of team skills as a function of type of training. J. Appl. Psychol. 50, 2,,102-8.

Kalra, S.K., 1983 : Case method and syndicate in management training. In R.K. Mishra and S. Ravishankar (eds.) : Management Development and Training in Public Enterprises. Ajanta Publications, New Delhi, 369 -378.

Keisler, C.A., Collins, B.E., and Miller, N., 1969 : Attitude Change. New York : Wiley.

Kennedy, J.B., 1970 : Use of audio-visual techniques in training the hardcore. Train. Develop. J., 24, 2, 30-33.

Khandelwal, A.K., 1983 : Management training in public sector banks. In R.K. Mishra and S. Ravishankar (eds) : Management Development and Training in Public Enterprises. Ajanta Publications, New Delhi, 253-268.

Khandelwal, N.M., 1983 : Training for internal auditors in public enterprises. In R.K. Mishra and S. Ravishankar (eds) : Management Development and Training in Public Enterprises. Ajanta Publications, 217-224.

Kinkade, R.G., and Kidd, J.S., 1962 : The use of an operational game as a method of task familiarization, Journal of Applied Psychology, 46, 1-10

Klaus, D.J., Grant, L.D., and Glaser, R., 1967 : Increasing team proficiency through training : Supervisory furnished reinforcement in team training U.S. Govt. Res. Develop. Rep. 67,6,22.

Klein, A.R., 1978 : Examination of Hackman of Oldham job Enrichment theory. Dissertation Abstracts International, 38, 9, March, 1978, 4519-B.

Kline, B.W., 1969 : Mind, Inc. system approach to training hardcore employables. Train-Develo. J., 23, 9, 18-21.

Koffka, Kurt, 1935 : Principles of Gestalt Psychology. Harcourt, Brace, 110. in Gordon L Lippitt, Leslie E. This, and Robert G. Bidwell (eds): Optimizing Human Resources : Readings in individual and organization development. Addison-Wesley Publishing Company, Reading, Mass :p.46.

Kohn, V., Parker, T.C., 1969 : Some guidelines for evaluating management development seminars. Train. Develop.J., 23, 7, 18-23.

Kolb, D.A., Winter, S.K., and Berlew, D.E., 1968 : Self directed change : Two studies. J. Appl. Behav. Sci., 4,4, 453-72.

Konwin, V. 1967 : A motivational approach to training. Train. Develop. J., 21, 3, 26-31.

Kraut, A.I., 1975 : Predicting turnover of employees from measured job attitudes. Organizational Behaviour and Human Performance, 13, 233-243.

Lawler, E.E. and Porter, L.W., 1967 : Antecedent attitudes of effective managerial performance. Organizational Behaviour and Human Performance, May, 127-147.

Lee, J.A., 1968 : Developing managers in developing countries. Harvard Bus. Rev., 46, 6, 55-65.

Lofkowitz, J., 1970 : Effect of training on the productivity and tenure of sewing machine operators, J. Appl. Psychol., 54, 81-86.

Leifer, M.S., and Newstorm, J.W., 1980 : Solving the transfer of training problems. Train. Dev. J., 34, 42-46.

Likert, R., 1967 : The Human Organization : Its management and value. MC. Graw Hill.

Lippitt. G.L., This, L.E.,Bidwell, R.G., Jr., 1971 : Optimizing Human Resources : Reading in Individual and Organizational Development.

Locke, E.A., 1966 : A closer look at level of aspiration as a training procedure : A re-analysis of Fryers data. J. Appl. Psychol., 50, 5, 417-20.

Locke, E.A., 1967 : The motivational effect of knowledge of results : Knowledge or goal setting? J. Appl. Psycol., 51, 324-29.

Locke, E.A., et. al. 1968 : Goals and intentions as mediators or the effects of monetary incentives on behaviour. J. Appl. Psychol., 52, 104-9.

Locke, E.A., 1969 : The relationship of satisfaction to performance: A theoretical model. Presented at Mid-western Psychol. Assoc.

Lubin, B., Zuckerman, M., 1969 : Level of emotional arousal in laboratory training, J. Appl. Behav. Sci., 5,4,482-90.

Lundberg., C.C., 1966 : Management development refocussed. Personnel Admin., 29, 1, 39-48.

Lynton, R.P., and Pareek, U., 1967 : Training for Development Homewood, III., : Dorsey.

Mager, R.F. and Pipe, P., 1969 : Analyzing performance problems. Palo Alto, Calif. Fearon Publishers.

Mahler, Walt, and Wrightnour, W., 1973 : Executive Community Dow Jones - Irwin Inc.

Main, E.D., 1968 : A nation-wide evaluation of M.D.T.A. Institutional job training. J. Hum. Res., 3,2, 159-170.

Margarison, C. and Kakabadse, A., 1985 : Developing Managers: Is what they need what they get? HRD ; Facts and figures: Training, January, p. 80.

Marlett, G.A., and Gordon, J.R., 1980 : Determinants of relapse : Implications for the maintenance of behavioural change. In behavioural medicine changing health life styles, P.O., Davidson, S.M. Davidson, (ed). New York : Burmmer/ Mazell, 410-52.

Marx, R.D. 1982 : Relapse prevention for managerial training . A model for maintenance of behaviour change. Acad. Manage. Re., 7, 433-41.

Mayo, G.D., and Longo, A.A., 1966 : Training time and programmed instruction. J. Appl. Psychol, 50, 1, 1-4.

Mayo, G.D., 1969 : Programmed instruction in technical training. Research Report, Naval Personnel Research Activity, San Diego.

Mc Cord, H.S., Jr., 1968 : The universality of learning Principles. Train-Develop. J., 22, 9, 48-51.

Mehrabian, A., 1970 : Tactics of social influence. Englewood Cliffs. N.J.Prentice-Hall.

Mehtani, P., 1985 : Work value orientation : A cross cultural study. Indian J. Appl. Psychol., 22, 2, July, 63-65.

Merri, Howard and Marting Elizabeth (eds.) 1970 : Developing Executive Skills : New pattern of management growth. D.B. Taraporewala Sons and Co. Private Ltd., Bombay.

Meyers, G.E., et. al., 1969 : Effect of feedback on interpersonal sensitivity in laboratory training group. J. Appl. Behav. Sci., 5,2, 175-86.

Mezof, B. 1982 : Cognitive style and inter personal behaviour : A review with implications for human relations training. Group Organ. Stud. Amherst, Mass : Sage.

Michalak, D.F., 1981 : The neglected half of training. Train. Dev. J., 35, 22-28.

Miles, M.B., 1965 : Changes during and following laboratory training : Clinical experimental study. J. Appl. Behav. Sci., 1, 215-42.

Miller, R.D., 1969 : A systems concept of training. Train. Develop. J., 23, 4, 4-15.

Miller, R.B., 1973 : Ask Analysis : Sources and Futures. Improving Human Performance, 2, pp. 5-27.

Minocha, O.P. 1983 : Determining training needs of public enterprises. In R.K. Mishra and S. Ravishankar (eds) : Management Development and Training in Public Enterprises. Ajanta Publications, New Delhi, 443-454.

Mishra, R.K., and Ravishankar, S.,(eds), 1983 : Designing and implementing an O.D., and training strategy for public sectors. Management Development and Training in Public Enterprises. Ajanta Publications, New Delhi, 491-508.

Mohan, J and Jahangiri, H., 1985 : Managerial effectiveness in relation to occupational goal values. Ind.J.Appl. Psychol., 22, 2, July, 70-75.

Mollenkopf, W.D., 1969 : Some results of three basic skills training programmes in an industrial setting. J. Appl. Psychol. 153, 5, 343-47.

Moore, L.F., 1967 : Business games versus cases and tools of learning. Train-Develo. J., 21, 10, 13-23.

Morrison, J.H., 1969 : M-Scale : Encounter With Reality. Train. Develop. J., 23, 10, 20-21.

Murphy, J.P., 1969 : Minority group training in similar companies. Train. Develop. J, 23, 1, 10-13.

Nadler, E.B., and Flink, S.L., 1970 : Impact of laboratory training on socio-political ideology. J. Appl. Behav. Sci., 6, 79-92.

Naylor, J.C., and Briggs, G.E., 1965 : Team training effectiveness under various conditions. J. Appl. Psychol., 49, 4, 223-29.

Noble, G., 1969 : A study of the relationship between ability performance, attitudes, inclinations, and speed of progress using intrinsic programme instruction. Programme Learn, Education Tech. 6, 109-21.

O'Brien, G., Fiedler, F., Hewtt, T., 1971 : The effect of programmed culture training upon performance of volunteer medical teams in Central America, Hum. Relation 24, 209-31.

Odiorne, G.S., 1985 : Human resource strategies for the 80s. Training, January, 47-51.

O' Rourke, P., and Castelli, J.A., 1969 : A follow-up study on supervisor training. Train. Develop. J., 23, 10, 32-41.

Pareek, Udai, 1983 : Educational and training activities in organizations. In R.K. Mishra and S. Ravishankar ; Management Development in Public Enterprises, Ajanta Publications, New Delhi, 1983, 41-62.

Pareek, Udai, 1983 : Trevacube : A comprehensive framework for training evaluation. In R.K. Mishra and S. Ravishankar (eds) : Management Development and Training in Public Enterprises. Ajanta Publications, New Delhi, 353-368.

Parmeswaran, E.G., 1983 : Psychological Bases ot Management Training : In R.K. Mishra and S.Ravishankar (eds) : Management Development in Public Enterprises. Ajanta Publications, New Delhi, 71-72.

Parmeswaran, E.G., 1983: Psychological Bases of Management Training. In R.K. Mishra and S. Ravishankar (eds.) : Management Development and Training in Public Enterprises. Ajanta Publications, New Delhi.

Patten, T.H., Jr., and Clark, G., Jr., 1968 : Literacy training and job placement of hardcore unemployed Negroes in Detroit. J. Hum. Res., 3, 1, 25-46.

Patten, J.H., Jr., and Stermer, 1969 : Training foremen in work standards. Train. Develop. J., 23, 11, 25-37.

Pikas, A., 1967 : Comparison between traditional and programmed learning as a function of the contents of the comparison test. Progr. Learn. Educ. Tech., 4, 270-83.

Porter, L.W., and Lawler, E.E., 1968 : Managerial Attitudes and Performance. Homewood, III : Dorsey.

Porter, L.W., and Steers, R.M., 1973 : Organizational, work, and personal factors in employee turnover and absenteeism. Psychological Bulletin, 80, 161-176.

Prakash, Om, 1983 : A case for vestibule training in public enterprises. In R.K. Mishra and S. Ravishankar (eds) : Management Development and Training in Public Enterprises, Ajanta Publications, New Delhi, 393-402.

Prakash, J., 1983 : Training for monitoring managerial performance in public enterprises. In R.K. Mishra and S. Ravishankar (eds) : Management Development and Training in Public Enterprises. Ajanta Publications, New Delhi, 189-298.

Pratap, S. and Srivastava, S.K., 1985 : A comparative study of job satisfaction and organization climate in private and public textile industries. Indian Journal of Applied Psychology 22, 1, January, 5-9.

Purcell R., and Webster, R, 1969 : 196 men find a chance : In D.B. Doeringer (ed.) : Programmes to employ the disadvantaged. Englewood Cliffs, N.J.Prentice-Hall.

Quakenboss, T.C., 1969 : White collar training takes many forms. Train. Develop. J. 23, 4, 16-27.

Rabinowitz., S., 1980 : Towards a developmental model of job involvement. Dissert. Abst. Int., 40, 8, Feb., 4008-B-4009-B.

Rao, G.V.S., and Ganguli, T., 1972 : Job satisfaction of highly skilled personnel : A test of the generality of the two-factor theory. Indian Journal of Applied Psychology, 9 ,1, January.

Reddin, W.J., 1967 : The 3-D management style theory. Train. Develop. J., 21,4,8-17.

Reddin, W.J., 1968 : The 3-D-organizational effectiveness program. Train. Develop. J., 22, 3, 22-29.

Reddin, W.J., 1969 : What's wrong with style theories? Train. Develop. J., 23, 8, 14-17.

Raghavachari, V.P., 1983 : Towards an educational policy for training public enterprise managers. In R.K. Mishra and S. Ravishankar (eds) : Management Development and Training in Public Enterprises, Ajanta Publications, New Delhi, 379-392.

Raghaviah, Y., 1983 : Training Organization for public enterprise managers : Problems and prospects. In R.K. Mishra and S. Ravishankar (eds.) : Management Development and Training in Public Enterprises. Ajanta Publications, New Delhi, 83-96.

Raia, A.P., 1966 : A study of the educational value of business games. J. Bus. 39, 339-52.

Raman, M.V.V., 1983 : Management training and industrial productivity. In R.K. Mishra and S. Ravishankar (eds.) : Management Development and Training in Public Enterprises. Ajanta Publications, New Delhi, 163-182.

Ramu, S.S., 1983 : Evaluation of Public enterprises. In R.K. Mishra and S. Ravishankar (eds) : Management Development and Training in Public Enterprises. Ajanta Publications, New Delhi, 317-352.

Ramu, S.S., 1983 : Personnel management in public sector in India. In R.K. Mishra and S. Ravishankar (eds) : Management Development and Training in Public Enterprises. Ajanta Publications, New Delhi, 299-316.

Rao, V.R., 1983 : Training and Developing women executives in public enterprises. In R.K. Mishra and S. Ravishankar (eds) : Management Development and Training in Public Enterprises. Ajanta Publications, New Delhi 269-278.

Ravishankar, S., and Mishra, R.K. (eds), 1983 : Audio-visual technology - Its role in training public enterprise managers. Management Development and Training in Public Enterprises. Ajanta Publications, New Delhi, 509.

Rawls, J.R., Perry O., and Timmons, E.O., 1966 : A comparative study of conventional instruction and individual programme instruction in the college classroom. J. Appl. Psychol., 50, 5, 388-91.

Rawls, J.R., and Rawls D.J., 1968 : Evaluation of closed circuit television in teaching educational psychology. Psychol. Rep. 22, 1041-44.

Roberts, K.H., 1970- : On looking at an elephant : An evaluation of cross cultural research related to organizations. Psychol. Bull.

Rock, R.T., Duva, J.S., and Murray, J.E., 1967 : Training by television, television recordings, and conventional classroom procedures. U.S. Govt. Res. Develop. Rep. 67, 1, 16.

Rodgers, C.R.P., (1966) : Management development in overseas branches - One company's programme. Personnel J., 43, 3, 62-66.

Rokeach, M. 1968 : Beliefs, Attitudes, and Values. San Fransisco : Jossey - Bass.

Rosen, N.A., Williams, L.K., and Flotmen, F.F., 1965 : Motivational Constraints in an industrial training programme. Personnel Psychol. 18, 1, 65-80.

Rosen, H., 1968 : On the job orientation of unemployed Negro skill canter trainees and their supervisors. Wayne State Univ., Deptt. Psychol.

Rothkopf, E.Z., 1963 : Some observations on predicting instructional effectiveness by simple inspection. Journal of Programmed Instructions, 2, 19-20.

Rubin, I., 1967 : The reduction of prejudice through laboratory training. J.Appl. Behav. Sci. 3, 1, 29-50.

Rummler, G.A., 1976 : The performance audit. Training and Development Handbook (2nd ed.) Mc Graw Hill, N.Y.

Salas, E.A., 1985 : Facilitating and hindering, factors in implementing managerial technology : A socio-technical system process. Dissertation Abstracts International, 45, 8, 2725-B.

Salvendy, G. and Boydstun, 1980 : A conceptual approach to development and validation of hierarchical acquisition in psychomotor performance. Jpn. Psychol. Res., 22, 64-71.

Schramm, W., 1968 : The research on programmed instruction : An annotated bibliography. Washington, D.C. : 1964, No. 35, Dept. HEW.

Schuster, D.H., 1968 : Evaluation of a new hybrid in programmed instruction. J. Appl. Psychol., 52, 4, 309-12.

Schwart, H.A., and Haskell, R.J., Jr., 1964 : A study of computer assisted instruction in industrial training. J. Appl. Psychol., 50, 5, 360-63.

Schwartz, H.A., and Long, H.S., 1967 : A study of remote industrial training via computer assisted instruction. J. Appl. Psychol., 51, 1, 11-16.

Schwartz, F.C., Stilwell, W.P., and Scanlan, B.K., 1968 : Effects of management development on manager behaviour and subordinate perception. Train. Develop. J., 22, 5, 24-30.

Scott, L.C., 1970 : The economic effectiveness of on the job training : The experience of the Bureau of Indian Affairs in Okalahoma. Industr. Labour Relat. Rev., 23, 2, 220-36.

Seidel, R.J., and Hunter, H.G., 1968 : The application of theoretical factors in teaching problem solving by programmed instruction. U.S. Govt. Res. Develo. Report., 68, 14, 24.

Shaw, M.E., and Wright, J.M., 1967 : Scales for the Measurement of attitudes. New York : Mc Graw-Hill.

Schendel, J.D., and Hagnmen, J.D., 1982 : On sustaining procedural skills over a prolonged retention interval. J. Appl. Psychol., 67, 605-10.

Schoombee, Desire, 1980 : Organizational climate as determining factor in managerial training. Dissertation Abst. International 40, 8, February. 4010-B.

Schwab, Donald P, et al., 1971 : " A test of the adequacy of the two factor theory as a predictor of self-report performance effects, "Personnel Psychology, 293-300.

Sikula, Andrew F., 1971 : Values and value systems : Important relationship to managerial and organizational behaviour. J. Psychol., 78, 277-286.

Sharma, A.K., 1983 : On the job training as a method of management development : The experience of British nationalized industry. In R.K. Mishra and S. Ravishankar (eds) : Management Development and Training in Public Enterprises. Ajanta Publications, New Delhi 429-442.

Singh, P. and Pant, K., 1983 : Public Enterprises in India - A case study of managerial helplessness. In R.K. Mishra and S. Ravishankar (eds.) : Management Development and Training in Public Enterprises. Ajanta Publications, New Delhi, 471-490.

Saha, B.K., and Dutta, O.N., 1983 : Training in materials management with reference to public enterprises. In R.K. Mishra and S. Ravishankar (eds.) : Management Development and Training in Public Enterprises. Ajanta Publications, New Delhi, 239-252.

Singh, P.N., 1986 : HRD World. Indian Journal of Training and Development, Indian Society for Training and Development, XVI, 4, October-December, 222-23.

Slocum, J.W., Jr., 1968 : Sensitivity and self-awareness changes : An empirical investigation. Train. Develo. J., 22, 9, 38-47.

Smith, R.C., Jr., 1968 : Innovations in teaching and training, Detroit, Mich : American Data Processing.

Smith, Judson, 1978 : Selecting and Developing only the best employees. Training, 15, 9, September, 21-24.

Solie, R.J., 1968 : Employment effects of retraining the unemployed. Industr. Labor. Relat. Rev. 21,2, 210-25.

Soliman, H.M., 1969 : The motivation hygiene theory of job attitudes : An empirical investigation and attempt to reconcile both the one and the two-factor theory of job attitudes. Dissertation Abstracts International, 1970, 31, 2, 943-B.

Srivastava, S.K., 1985 : A comparative study of job satisfaction among private and public sector employees with special reference to achievement motivation. Indian Journal of Applied Psychology, 22, 1, January, 10-12.

Steele, F.I., 1968 : Personality and the "Laboratory Style". J. Appl. Behav. Sci., 4, 1, 25-46.

Steinmetz, L.L., and Patten, R.J., 1967 : Enthusiasm, interest and learning : The results of game training. Train. Develop. J.21, 4, 26-36.

Stoller, F., 1968 : Use of Video Tape (focused feedback) in group counselling and group therapy. J. Res.Develo. Educ., 1,2, 20-43.

Stone. E.F., 1977 : Some personality correlates of perceptions and reactions of task characteristics. Working Paper, Purdue University.

Stone, E.F., 1979 : Field independence and perceptions of task characteristics : A laboratory investigation. Journal of Applied Psychology, 64, 305-310.

Stromsdorfer, E.W., 1968 : Determinants of economic success in retraining the unemployed : The West Virginia Experience. J. Hum. Res. 3, 2, 139-58.

Stufflebeam, D.L., 1977 : Working paper on needs assessment. Kalamazoo, M.I. : Evaluation Centre, Western Michigan University.

Taylor, F.W., 1911 : The Principles of Scientific Management. New York : Harper.

Tennenbaum, L.R., Weschler, I.R., and Massarik, F., 1961 : Leadership and Organization : A behavioural science approach. Mc Graw Hill, New York, 132.

This, Leslie E., and Lippitt. Gordon., L, 1971 : Learning Theories and Training; An overview of learning theory implications for the training director. In Gordon L. Lippitt. Leslie E. This, and Robert G.Bidwell, Jr. (eds.) : Optimizing Human Resources Readings: In Individual and Organizational Development. Addison-Wesley Publishing Company, Reading, Massachusetts. 41-59.

Thorley, S., 1969 : Evaluating an in company management training program. Train. Develop. J;, 23, 9, 49-51.

Tiffin, J. and Mc Cormic, E.J., 1958 : Industrial Psychology, 4th ed., Prentice Hall, Englewood Cliffs.

Tubiana, J.H., and Ben-Shakhar, G., 1982 : An objective group questionnaire as a substitute for a personal interview in the prediction of success in military training in Israel. Personnel Psychol., 35, 349-57.

Turner, A.N. and Lawrence, P.R., 1965 : Industrial Jobs and the Worker. Cambridge, MA : Harward University, Graduate School of Business Administration.

Ullman, L.P., and Krasner, L.(eds.) 1965 : Case studies in Behaviour Modification. New York : Holt, Rinchart and Winston.

Underwood, W.J., 1965 : Evaluation of Laboratory method training Train. Directors J., 19, 5, 34-40.

Utgaard. S.B. and Davis, R.V., 1970 : The most frequently used training techniques. Train. Develop. J., 24, 2, 40-43.

Valiquet, M.I., 1968 : Individual change in a laboratory program, J. Appl. Behav. Sci. 4, 313-26.

Van Brunt, R.E., 1969 : Unexpected results when training the disadvantaged. Train. Develop. J., 23, 10 22-27.

Venkataratnam, C.S., 1983 : Developing Executive skills in public enterprise managers. In R.K. Mishra and S. Ravishankar, (eds.) 1983 : Management Development and Training in Public Enterprises. Ajanta Publications, New Delhi, 113-128.

Viteles, M.S., 1969 : Long Range Impact on Managerial Attitude and Behaviour : A follow-up survey. Philadelphia : Bell.

Walsh, P., Antoineth, J.A., and Thayer, P.W., 1965 : An industry wide study of programmed instruction, J., Appl. Psychol., 49, 1, 61-73.

Whitlock, G.H., 1967 : Programmed Learning : Some non-Confirming Results. Training. Develop. J.,21,6,11-13.

Wiener, E.L., and Attwood, D.A., 1968 : Training for vigilance combined cueing and knowledge of results. J. Appl. Psychol;, 52, 6, 474-79.

Wool, H., and Flyer, E.S., 1969 : Project 100,000. In D.B. Doeringer(ed). : Programs to employ the disadvantaged, Englewood Cliffs, N.J.Prentice-Hall.

Zand, E.E., Steele, F.I., Zalkind, S.S., 1969 : The impact of an organizational development program on perception of inter-personal, group, and organization functioning, J. Appl. Behav. Sci 5, 3, 393-410.

Zaner, T., 1968 : Action research in management development. Train. Develop., J., 22,6, 28-33.

Zink, D.L., 1982 : Standards for time taken in self-paced training presented at Ann. Meet. Hum. Factors Soc., Seattle.

INDEX

Achievement value, 93
Achievement value inventory, 97
Administration Model, 12
Adult learning, 24
Age, 91
Amarchand, 68
Analysis of data, 98
factor, 98
correlation, 98
multiple regression, 98
graphical representations, 98
engineers, 120
social welfare officers, 120
Attitude towards training, 121
Attitude towards training questionnaire, 99
Background information form, 94
Basic encounter and personal growth training, 29
Boyd, 39
broad areas of Indian studies, 68
Compbell, 38
Clark, 66
Classification of management development, 37
Cognitive approach, 36
Correlation of achievement value with attitude towards training, 124
Correlation of job satisfaction and quality of work life with attitude with training, 129
Correlation of motivating potential with attitude towards training, 124
Correlation of occupational aspiration, 121, 122, 148-49
Cross-cultural training, 30
Data collection, 97-98
Demotivating climate, 130
Description of instruments, 94
Dholakia, 72
Doraiswami, 66, 68
Educational level, 91
Effect of individual characteristics on job enrichment, 20
Eigen values, percentage and variance and cumulative percentage of factors, 104, 105
Elliss, 39
Engineers, 125
organizational image, 128
development opportunities, 128
organizational work style, 129
motivating work climate, 129
age, 134
no. of workers supervised, 134
educational level, 134
experience, 134
training effectiveness, 137
personal growth and development, 137
competence, 137
Experience, 91
Factor scores, dimensions of training experience, 108-11

Fernades, 70
Functional areas of MD, 71
Future exploration, 165
Gains from training, 143
Ganguli, 74
General management programmes, 43
Growth-Need Strength, 20, 63
Handa, 74
Humanistic-Organismic approach, 159
Human relations programme, 43
Human Resource Development, 3, 5, 9, 46-78
    models and theories, 48
    attitude theory, 52
    Motivation theory, 52
    behaviour modification, 53
    individual differences, 55
    general system theory, 56
    interventional theory, 57
    models of management of development, 58
    replase prevention model, 58
    multi-faced system, 59
Hypothesis-I, 81
Hypothesis 2 of Engineers and SWO's, 82, 123
Hypothesis 3 of Engineers and SWO's, 125
Hypothesis 4 of Engineers and SWO's 83, 125
Hypothesis 5, 85, 134
Hypothesis-6, 85
Independent variables, 92
    background, 92
    psychological, 92
    dependent, 92
    occupation aspiration, 92
Indian studies, 67
Insincerity, 130
Instruments, 94
Integrated model, 16
Job characteristics approach, 19
Job characteristics, 62
Job design and job aids, 61
Job diagnostic survey, 63
Job enlargement, 61
Job enrichment, 62
Job involvement inventory, 95
Job involvement, 93, 122
Job satisfaction, 83, 93
Job satisfaction scale, 97
Kazmi, 76
Khandelwal, 72
Klien, 83
Laboratory education, 41
Leader behaviour description questionnaire, 38
Learning theories and management development programme, 22
    behaviourist school, 23
    gestalt school, 23
    functionalist school, 23
    mathematical school, 23
    current learning theory schools, 23
Management Development, 9
    models of, 11
Mean of gains from training, motivation for personal growth, 151
Mean of personal growth, competence and development, 150
Mean of training effectiveness, 149
Mehtani, 82
Minocha, 74
Monappa, 76
Motivating environment, 130
Motivation for personal growth, 143
Motivation potential, 125
Motivation for personal growth, 121
Motivating potential, 93
Motivating potential scale, 97
National Institute of Training for Public Enterprises, 74
No. of factors (Engineers), 106
    Social Welfare Officers, 107
Occupational aspiration, 81
Occupational aspiration inventory, 94
Occupational aspiration, 120
Organizational climate, 84
Organizational Development, 4, 6, 9
Organizational strategies, 130
Organization I, 88
Organization II, 88
Parmeswaran, 66
Pay scales, 91
Personal growth and development, 121
Phases of a training development System, 18

Prakash, 73
Problem solving and decision making, 43
Problem-solving model, 15, 16
Product moment correlation co-efficient, 117
Programmed and Computer assisted instructions, 30, 33
    programmed, 30
    orientation training, 33
    sales training, 34
    training through television, 34
    team training, 34
    simulation, 35
    speciality programme, 35
Psychological theories of MD training, 25-27
Quality circles, 85
Quality of work life questionnaire, 95
Quality of work life, 63, 84, 93
Quality of work, 20
Raman, 70
Ravishankar, 75
Recommendations, 162
References, 166-89
Regression analysis of competence and occupational aspiration, 145
Regression analysis of competence, 140
Regression analysis of gains from training, 141
Regression analysis of motivation for personal growth, 142, 146
Regression analysis of training effectiveness, 144
Reliability, 95
Review of literature, 67
Sample selection and sample characteristics, 86
Scanlan, 38
Schwartz, 38
Scoring, 113
Seven psychological correlates, 165
Sex, 91
Social Welfare Officers, 87
Social Welfare Officers, 130
    motivating work climate, 130
    developmental opportunities, 131
    organizational image and strategies, 131-32
    fairness, 132
    work values, 132
    insincerity, 132
    organizational strategies, 132
    age, 135
    sex, 135
    pay scale, 135
    educational level, 136
Stilwel, 38
Synthesizing model, 13, 14
Television and telephone training, 29
Training and Development Journal, 72
Training effectiveness, 121
Training experience, 86, 93
Training experience Questionnaire, 94
Transformation matrix of Engineers and Social Welfare Officers, 112
United Nations, 73
Unrotated factor matrix for attitude towards training, 100,102
Validity, 95
    convergent, 95-96
    discriminant, 96
    construct, 96
Varimax rotated factor matrix for attitude towards training, 101, 103
Workers supervised, 91
Work values, 130